JUMPING INTO
CIVIC LIFE

Stories of Public Work from Extension Professionals

Edited by
Scott J. Peters, Theodore R. Alter, and Timothy J. Shaffer

Jumping into Civic Life: Stories of Public Work from Extension Professionals
is published by the Kettering Foundation Press. The interpretations and
conclusions contained in the book represent the views of the authors. They
do not necessarily reflect the views of the Charles F. Kettering Foundation,
its directors, or its officers.

For information about permission to reproduce selections from this book,
write to:

Permissions
Kettering Foundation Press
200 Commons Road
Dayton, Ohio 45459

This book is printed on acid-free paper.
First edition, 2018
Manufactured in the United States of America

ISBN: (print) 978-1-945577-37-6
ISBN: (ePDF) 1-945577-38-3
ISBN: (ePUB) 1-945577-39-0

Library of Congress Control Number: 2018933682

Cover design by Alyssa M. Gurklis

Artwork on page 106:
Norman Rockwell Visits a County Agent by Norman Rockwell
Printed by permission of the Norman Rockwell Family Agency
Copyright ©1948 the Norman Rockwell Family Entities

While I am sure that in the present appreciation of "facts" we have the most hopeful promise for our confessedly fumbling world, the most needed corrective for certain attitudes of mind into which we have fallen, while I know from experience that we often waste time in conference arguing about things that are ascertainable, still there are several points which must be remembered: it is of equal importance with the discovery of facts to know what to do with them; our job is to apportion, not usurp, function (the "people" have a place, what is it?); and also we must warn ourselves that a little of the ready reliance on the expert comes from the desire to waive responsibility, comes from the endless evasion of life instead of an honest facing of it. The expert is to many what the priest is, someone who knows absolutely and can tell us what to do. The king, the priest, the expert, have one after the other had our allegiance, but so far as we put any of them in the place of ourselves, we have not a sound society and neither individual nor general progress.

Mary Parker Follett
Creative Experience, 1924

Table of Contents

Acknowledgments

Civic life is difficult. It can also be frustrating, painful, and risky. Given these realities, why do people jump into it? *compell — force — coerce*

One answer is that they are compelled to do so, by anger or love. Or more likely, by both. While people may jump into civic life out of anger, their anger usually emerges from a sense that someone or something they love is being harmed or disrespected.

That's certainly the case with us. As academic professionals, we have jumped into civic life—both on and off our campuses—out of anger over the ways that people, places, and processes we love are being harmed or disrespected. This book is one product of our work as publicly engaged scholars. Since such work is inherently collaborative, we owe many people acknowledgments of gratitude for their contributions, support, and inspiration.

First, we want to express our gratitude for the stories, insights, and wisdom we were fortunate to hear and receive from dozens of our Extension and land-grant colleagues who participated with us in the Kettering Foundation research exchanges that led to the publication of this book. The time we spent together included a good deal of truth-telling, much of which was troubling and challenging. Thankfully, we managed to keep our main focus on promising possibilities, revealed through first-person stories of their (and our) lives and work. Together we generated more than a thousand pages of transcripts of such stories that we will continue to draw on and learn from for years to come. We are especially grateful that eight of our Extension colleagues were willing to have their stories published. We thank Carmen DeRusha, Janet Ayres, Joe Sumners, Katrina Easley, Bill McGowan, Daryl Buchholz, Sue Williams, and Jan Hartough for their generosity and boldness. Their voices and stories will remain with us always, as sources of inspiration and hope.

Second, we are deeply grateful for the support and encouragement we received from the Kettering Foundation, especially senior associate Alice Diebel. We owe Alice more than we probably know, not only for believing in our project—which is much larger than this book, and will include many more products—but also for contributing to it in many substantive ways, and for putting up with it and us as our timeframe for completion stretched out much longer than we originally anticipated. We deeply value the time we spent with her. With respect to the Kettering Foundation itself, we feel compelled to speak a truth: it is the *only* organization in the entire country that offers sustained opportunities for Extension and land-grant professionals to explore the civic dimensions of their work. It would be impossible for us to overemphasize how important that has been, and still is.

Finally, we owe an unpayable debt of gratitude to a set of Extension and land-grant leaders from the 19th and 20th centuries whose bold democratic vision continues to inspire and agitate us every day. Liberty Hyde Bailey, Minnie Price, Ruby Green Smith, M. L. Wilson, and countless others from those centuries were the original citizen professionals in the Extension and land-grant system. Like us, their lives and work weren't perfect. But they managed to establish a democratic tradition in our institutions, and gave us standards we strive to honor. Their civic commitments and aspirations live on, as the stories you will read in this book reveal. May they always.

Foreword

This book is a remarkable testament to the confidence its storytellers have in the people who live in the communities they serve. These stories are of Cooperative Extension agents—or educators, as they are now often referred to—and leaders who recognize that people have the inherent capacity to make significant differences in their collective lives. The authors of these narratives are pushing against the norm in Cooperative Extension, an institution that typically recognizes its role in the research university as that of transferring technical information to citizens, or of applying proven programs to communities. Unlike much of Cooperative Extension and other university systems, these authors recognize that difficult and persistent community problems are not easily addressed without citizens, and that applying a technical "fix" to people limits creative alternatives and further pushes citizens *out* of public life. What role is there for citizens if an expert has the answers? These democratically spirited agents have learned that they do not have all the answers and see their role as facilitating the public engagement of issues using a myriad of approaches to deal with the many problems of living in community.

The challenge, as the Kettering Foundation sees it, is that too often university outreach efforts come from an expert position bringing *service* learning to needy publics or *research* to communities that may be tired of being studied. What the extraordinary people in this collection of narratives do is value communities and the residents within them and see them as actors who *should* have a role in shaping their collective futures. They have used an *educational* approach that involves shared learning rather than a one-way transfer of scientific knowledge. The citizens these agents see have knowledge of what they value and want for their futures, capacities for deciding among alternatives, and assets to put to work. These Extension representatives understand that the university needs to align itself with what citizens see as their concerns rather than telling citizens what their concerns should be. They are learning as much as the people they are working with. The agent's educational role is around learning *with* diverse groups of citizens, in spaces filled with history and context, to understand and cocreate democratic approaches to community politics.

As a research organization, Kettering offers a lens for people who are trying to encourage more democratic approaches to politics. Kettering's approach to its work looks a lot like the shared learning model the Extension agents use in these narratives. Kettering does not have answers or fact sheets, but rather, poses questions that encourage groups to think about the nature of the politics they experience, work through what democracy could be in a variety of contexts, and listen carefully to what practitioners are learning. The foundation encourages democratic innovations in shared problem solving.

For these innovations to affect the politics of a community and shape a more democratic public life, institutions like universities need to see citizens as more than voters or as barriers to progress. By seeing them as the experts of their own lives and finding ways for people to hear diverse perspectives, Kettering asserts that decisions will be better informed, more cognizant of the valuable things one might lose in order to make progress, and more open to working across divisions. These innovations build the capacity of people to have stronger, democratic communities in a way that harkens back to an earlier mission of Extension as described by Tim Shaffer in the last chapter of this volume.

Democracy is an unfinished business and requires a level of uncertainty that a research university may not care to own. Therein lies the tension. What is the role of Cooperative Extension? Is it to build the capacity of citizens to shape their own communities and collective futures, or is it to deliver well-rehearsed programs? The experimenters in this volume find a way to blend the wisdom of community and the resources of the institution in a way that aligns them in their shared work of building stronger, democratic places.

Some of the specific wisdom we see from these authors relates directly to the Kettering Foundation's lens of inquiry. Carmen DeRusha sees that many communities are just "collections of individuals" but has confidence that they will develop as a community, able to deliberate and act on their own behalf. Janet Ayres sees Cooperative Extension not as the decision maker or recommender, but instead as a facilitator and relationship builder. More specific, Joe Sumners identifies difficult divisions that prevent people from working together—divisions of race and class. He sees Extension as the humble catalyst. Katrina Easley also recognizes the barriers race can play in preventing forward movement in community. She is optimistic about change, especially when young people get involved.

Bill McGowan recognizes the value of university-provided information, but sees it playing a role only when people start to talk about what concerns them. Daryl Buchholz sees university knowledge as important to the public good, but not as the answer. Sue Williams also identifies supporting community deliberation in decision making beyond sharing facts.

Finally, Jan Hartough clearly states that each situation is unique. If Extension is to cultivate and support citizen choice making about their own communities, then the role for Extension leaders is one of facilitation and guidance.

Kettering's enthusiasm for the innovative work of the authors results from their sense of tentativeness, their respect for the people they work with, their ability to blend what limited expertise they do have with the wisdom of the community, and their willingness to dive into politics. They are democratically minded professionals, working within a system that rightly avoids engaging in partisan politics. However, partisanship is *not* the kind of politics the agents in this volume care about. Rather, it is the difficult work of helping citizens in communities understand difference, struggle with ways to work through those differences, and make choices from among scarce resources on their own behalf. It is self-reliance and collective action both, a testament to our human potential in the face of difficulties.

Alice Diebel, Senior Associate
Kettering Foundation

Introduction

Making Democracy Work as It Should

by Scott J. Peters, Theodore R. Alter, and Timothy J. Shaffer

Whatever they may understand democracy to be, most people would likely agree that it isn't working as it should. This book is one product of several years of research on a particular aspect of this problem. We conducted it in collaboration with the Kettering Foundation of Dayton, Ohio.

As a research foundation, Kettering's work is focused on the question, "what does it take to make democracy work as it should?" In the foundation's view, democracy isn't just a system of government. It's not something we *have*; it's something we *do*, and it includes much more than voting in elections. It's a way of life that involves everyone as *citizens*, understood in an inclusive, nonlegal sense to mean active agents in the political process of self-government.

Democracy works as it should, Kettering Foundation research suggests, when people from a full range of backgrounds and identities have ample opportunity to come together in their own neighborhoods and communities to name, frame, deliberate about, and act on their common problems, pursue their aspirations, and shape their collective future on their own terms, through their own labor. More than just talk, such labor engages people in a cocreative, citizen-centered politics that produces things of public value. We can understand this kind of labor as *public work*, pursued in everyday life through a set of interrelated democratic practices.[1] Quoting Kettering Foundation's president, David Mathews, these practices include the following:

1. Naming problems to reflect the things people consider valuable and hold dear, not expert information alone.

2. Framing issues for decision making that not only takes into account what people value but also lays out all the major

options for acting fairly and with full recognition of the tension growing out of advantages and disadvantages of each option.

3. Making decisions deliberatively to move opinions from first impressions to more shared and reflective judgment.

4. Identifying and committing civic resources, assets that often go unrecognized and unused.

5. Organizing civic actions so they complement one another, which makes the whole of people's efforts more than the sum of the parts.

6. Learning as a community all along the way to keep up civic momentum.[2]

There are many forces at work in the world that hinder rather than support these democratic practices. One source of trouble has to do with professionals, and the institutions that employ them. That's our focus in this book.

THREE VIEWS OF PROFESSIONALS

Professionals are people with particular kinds of credentialed expertise. They include doctors, lawyers, scientists, teachers, journalists, social workers, and a host of other occupations. The institutions that employ them include hospitals, businesses, government agencies, schools, and nonprofits (or, as they are often called, NGOs—nongovernmental organizations).

In broad terms, there are three positions we can take on the question of whether, how, and for what purposes professionals should be engaged in civic life. The first, in essence, calls for professionals and their institutions to *stay out* of the work of naming, framing, and addressing the problems people face in their neighborhoods and communities. People who are not credentialed professionals not only *can* understand and address their problems on their own, those who hold this position may say, but in societies that aspire to be democratic, they *should*. Furthermore, advocates of this position may say, professionals and the institutions that employ them all too often act in ways that advance their own careers and biases, and/or the interests and agendas of the government and big corporations. They colonize civic life by taking on the civic work that citizen associations used to do. They sideline and disable citizens who are not paid professionals.[3] At their worst, they reinforce, reproduce, or worsen inequalities and various forms of discrimination and oppression.

A second position adds up, in essence, to a call for professionals to *take over* the work of naming, framing, and addressing people's problems, and for people who are not credentialed professionals to step aside. Only professionals have the kinds of knowledge and expertise that are needed to understand and address most of the problems we face today, those who hold this position may say. Furthermore, professionals are objective and disinterested. They're driven by science rather than politics. Instead of being focused on advancing their personal biases and self-interested agendas, they're focused on determining—through rigorous, objective, peer-reviewed research—what's best for the larger public good, and what actually works in pursuing it.

There are grains of truth in both of these positions. But there are married also serious problems. And to the extent to which they are espoused and followed in rigid, ideological ways that ignore or overly simplify the complexities of context and situation, they are not only unhelpful, but also, in many cases, destructive.

What we're interested in exploring is a third position that lies somewhere between these two extremes. Instead of calls for professionals to "Stay out!" or "Take over!" the position we're interested in centers on a conditional call that attends to the dynamics of particular contexts and situations: "If it makes sense and is possible, *jump in*—but be respectful, be humble, and be careful."

PROBLEMS IN AND OF DEMOCRACY

There are many things professionals who choose to jump into civic life and work in their capacity as professionals (we're not talking here about what they choose to do in their "off-hours") need to be respectful, humble, and careful about. They need to be respectful of lay citizens' experience, knowledge, and capacities. They need to be humble about their own expertise, informed by an awareness of its limits. And they need to be careful about the ways they name and address what David Mathews calls problems *in* democracy (that's another way of saying problems in our society).[4] Problems *in* democracy include such daunting societal challenges as climate change, poverty, mass incarceration, childhood obesity, access to and affordability of quality health care, gun violence, and opioid addiction. Such problems receive most of professionals' attention, and it's not hard to understand why. They have serious implications for things we have reason to value, such as clean water and air, health, economic prosperity, justice and equity, and the future of our children.

In the third position we support, the point isn't to encourage professionals to stop working on these problems or to abandon their expertise. Rather, it's to encourage them to take care that, as they do, they don't contribute to a different set of problems that David Mathews refers to as problems *of* democracy. Problems *of* democracy are related to the state of our civic life, to how well it's functioning. They include the sidelining of citizens from civic life; divisive and polarizing rhetoric; lack of opportunities for people to come together to talk about and work on the problems they're facing; lack of trust between people and institutions; lack of hope; a sense of powerlessness; and an ingrained belief that nothing can change.

In short, the danger we're pointing to is this: if professionals aren't respectful, humble, and careful, their practices can worsen problems *of* and *in* democracy by overestimating the value of their own expertise and underestimating the value of what lay citizens have to offer. Exploring this danger is an important—and highly complicated—project. But that exploration is not our main purpose in this book. Our purpose here is to help open our collective imagination to possibilities for professionals to jump into civic life in ways that support the task of making democracy work as it should.

EIGHT CHALLENGING SITUATIONS

Our source of inspiration and learning about these possibilities are stories professionals told us about their lives, and their practices and experiences as participants in public work. Captured in a set of eight oral history profiles that we edited from transcripts of narrative interviews, these life and practice stories humanize and contextualize work that all too often is only understood through theoretical and philosophical abstractions, broadbrush criticisms, or lists of "best practices." The stories professionals tell in these profiles are about challenging situations that take the form of mini-dramas: something happens to produce conflict and uncertainty, and the path forward is either unclear or disputed.

Here are thumbnail sketches of these situations, written from the vantage point of the professionals, all of whom are employed by or affiliated with the same institution: the national Cooperative Extension System ("Extension" for short):

- Carmen DeRusha, a newly hired professional employed by an institution that is funded almost entirely by tax dollars—Purdue Extension in Marion County, Indiana—starts knocking on doors in the Far East Side neighborhood of Indianapolis. She learns that there are 5,000 children in the neighborhood, but no recreational facilities. People tell her that they are worried about crime. They say they don't know which jurisdiction of the city police department is responsible for their area, and which of three local fire departments they're supposed to call if there's a fire. She meets with members of neighborhood organizations and tells them these and other things she has heard. They say, "Yes, yes, we know all of that. But we don't know what to do."

- A trustee from a township located near Lafayette, Indiana, tells Janet Ayres—a campus-based academic professional at Purdue University— that she's worried about the growth and development her township has been undergoing. Open spaces and farmland are being lost. Wetlands are being threatened. Decisions about growth are being made by people from the county and the city, leaving township residents with no voice. When Janet asks about organized groups of citizens in the township, the trustee tells her that, other than the volunteer fire department, there aren't any organized groups.

- Uniontown, a small town in the Black Belt region of Alabama, faces many economic and civic challenges that threaten its future. The mayor asks an administrator at Auburn University whether there is a way the university might help them. The administrator asks Joe Sumners, a campus-based academic professional with expertise in strategic planning, to lead a strategic planning process for the town. As he begins his work, he learns that there are no civic groups in Uniontown, and few opportunities for people to come together. Participants in the planning process decide to create a community development corporation (CDC) as a way for residents to start writing and receiving grants. Joe notices as the process moves forward that local residents expect the mayor, or outside experts like himself, to have all the answers to their problems. Then something unexpected happens: the mayor gets defeated in an election. The new mayor has no use for the strategic planning process the previous mayor had begun, or the CDC that was created. As a result, all the work Joe and his colleagues have done becomes irrelevant. They're back to square one.

- In Perry County, Alabama, Katrina Easley, who coordinates the county Extension office, is asked to coordinate and participate in an adult leadership class. The class, which includes a mix of white and black residents from many different backgrounds and occupations, begins discussing the current state of the county and ideas for how it might be improved. Soon after they start, disagreements begin to emerge. White members of the group push back against ideas for addressing African American community members' needs unless similar efforts are simultaneously made to address white community members' needs. As they struggle to find common ground, the project begins to fall apart.

- In the late 1990s, the Environmental Protection Agency (EPA) is threatened with a lawsuit if it doesn't hold the state of Delaware accountable for meeting the standards of the Clean Water Act. In 1999, the EPA reaches a settlement with the state. Delaware agrees to establish "total maximum daily loads" and "pollution control strategies" for all its impaired watersheds. With the Department of Natural Resources and Environmental Control and an organization called the Center for the Inland Bays taking on different tasks, work begins on the state's most impaired watershed: the Inland Bays. Bill McGowan, a county-based professional with the University of Delaware Extension Service, is invited to help design and organize action teams. He and his colleagues approach the task in what Bill refers to as the standard way: "Here is your committee; we need to get educated on what the issue is; we will develop recommendations, and then we will go out and inform folks about what we did." Then something happens that makes him realize that the standard way isn't working.

- Working as a campus-based Extension professional in Missouri, Daryl Buchholz, a soil scientist who later became the associate director of Cooperative Extension at Kansas State University, goes out to a rural community with a team of his colleagues. They give a set of presentations to farmers who are struggling to figure out how they are going to change the way they farm in order to comply with new conservation requirements. Reflecting on their presentations while on the way back to campus, Daryl says to his colleagues, "All we did was stand up in front of that crowd and tell them what their problems are. They all know what their problems are. What they're looking for are solutions to those problems. We have got to reorient the way we are approaching this whole thing, to help them address their problems. Not to hold up flags and say, 'This is going to be a problem if you go *this* route, and this is going to be a problem if you go *that* route.' " In response, some of his colleagues say that they think that what they did was the best they could do. Daryl tells them that he doesn't believe that's true.

- In the late 1970s and early 1980s, Oklahoma experiences a major farm crisis. Because of her expertise in financial and resource management, Sue Williams, a campus-based Extension professional at Oklahoma State University, is asked to contribute to work that is being done in agricultural economics to address the crisis. Because the issue is about much more than financial management, and because it's charged with powerful emotions, Sue and her colleagues struggle to figure out what they should do. There is a lot of blaming and frustration, and an expectation that Extension should not try to be "unbiased," but instead serve as an advocate for the farm sector. All this challenges Sue and her colleagues to determine what the appropriate role of professionals who are employed by a land-grant institution should be when addressing a difficult, emotionally charged issue. Sue figures out that she could provide factual information. But she admits that she has no clue how—or whether—she and her colleagues should try to address the emotional aspects of the issue.

- In January 2007, a small, upscale resort town in Michigan called Grand Haven experiences problems related to an overpopulation of deer. The city holds what turns out to be a contentious, highly polarized public forum on the issue. Neighbors and friends yell at each other. After the forum nothing much is done to follow up, and anger over the issue continues to simmer. A local agricultural Extension agent calls Jan Hartough, a state specialist with the Michigan State University Extension Service, and Frank Fear, a campus-based faculty member and administrator, and asks them whether they could help the town figure out how to deal with the issue. They meet with town officials and come up with a plan. The town holds three community forums, and then appoints a task force to examine and make preliminary recommendations for what should be done about issues that surfaced during the forums. Everything seems to be progressing well until a member of the task force decides to write a letter to the editor in the local paper expressing her personal views about what should be done. Suddenly, the trust that had been built up collapses, and the task force is split into opposing camps.

To find out how and why these professionals got themselves into these situations, and what happened next, we need to read their profiles. We can use what we learn from them to expand our imagination about possibilities for professionals' constructive contribution to the task of making democracy work as it should. The stories in the profiles also enable us to learn from their experiences, as they recount what happened as they tried to work through or around the barriers they encountered.

In the remainder of this introduction, we do three things to help readers make sense of and learn from the stories in these profiles. First, we offer some background about Extension, the institution that all of the professionals we introduced above are either employed by or affiliated with. Second, we explain how and why we cocreated the profiles in this book with them. Finally, we offer a set of three interconnected tools readers can use to interpret the profiles and the stories they contain.

BUT FIRST . . .

Before we move on, we want to offer a foundational interpretive tool that helps us attend to a critically important issue about stories, and storytelling. The issue is named in the following passage from a book that was cowritten by several scholars who call themselves the Personal Narratives Group:

> When talking about their lives, people lie sometimes, forget a lot, exaggerate, become confused, and get things wrong. Yet they *are* revealing truths. These truths don't reveal the past "as it actually was," aspiring to a standard of objectivity. They give us instead the truths of our experiences. They aren't the result of empirical research or the logic of mathematical deductions. Unlike the reassuring Truth of the scientific ideal, the truths of personal narratives are neither open to proof nor self-evident. We come to understand them only through interpretation, paying careful attention to the contexts that shape their creation and to the world views that inform them.[5]

Far from being troubled by this passage, we're grateful to have it. We use it on a regular basis as a tool to enhance our attentiveness to the *experiential truths* the stories we read or hear might contain. Such truths, we must point out, are not always good. They can be dangerous. They can reinforce myriad forms of hatred and evil. But they can also be like diamonds, the precious gems that only storytelling—one of humanity's oldest and most important ways of knowing—can offer us.[6]

Oral historian Alessandro Portelli provides us with another way of being attentive to these truths when he teaches us to be mindful of the difference in storytelling between the "telling of the truth" and "the truth of the telling."[7] We should never let our rightful concern for the former get in the way of our ability to see the latter. For what we need to inspire and sustain us in our lives and work is never just "the facts" about what "actually" happened. We also need the deeper truths we can gain from hearing and telling stories about our experiences.

The profiles in this book are full of such truths.

SOME BACKGROUND ON EXTENSION

Because it's likely that most readers of this book have never heard of Extension, or are only familiar with one part of it, such as its 4-H program for youth, we'd like to offer some background. We hope what we provide here will be of use as an interpretive tool to help readers make sense of the stories the professionals in this book tell. And we hope readers will be able to learn from these stories, even if they have no interest in Extension.

Extension is a large institution that is more than 100 years old. It reaches into nearly every county in the nation. The majority of its budget comes from county, state, and federal tax dollars. It was officially established as the national Cooperative Extension System on May 8, 1914, when President Woodrow Wilson signed the Smith-Lever Act into law. Since then it has grown into a highly complex institution—or more accurately, a set of loosely coupled institutions. It's administered separately in each state by one or more of the nation's land-grant colleges and universities (there are more than 100 of such institutions), usually by a faculty member who is appointed as director and/or dean.

Extension's current annual budget is almost $2 billion. It has a staff of more than 2,000 campus-based academic professionals from many different disciplines and fields, across and beyond the social, biological, and natural sciences. It employs more than 8,000 community-based educators (variously called "Extension educators," "Extension agents," or "county agents") who work at approximately 2,900 county and regional offices.[8] Extension professionals pursue their work in six broad areas: agriculture; community and economic development; family and consumer sciences; leadership development; natural resources; and youth development.

If we want to explore Extension professionals' roles in supporting or hindering the task of making democracy work as it should, we need to attend to the issue of what its purposes have been and are understood to be, and how those purposes have been and are currently being pursued through Extension professionals' practices. Going back to Extension's founding legislation, the Smith-Lever Act, we don't find much text about why it was created, what purposes it was supposed to pursue, and how its professional staff were supposed to pursue them. Only two passages in the legislation say anything about these issues. One states that Extension staff will "aid in diffusing among the people of the United States useful and practical information on subjects relating to agriculture and home economics, and to encourage the application of the same." The other states that Extension work is to "consist of the giving of instruction and practical demonstrations in agriculture and home economics to persons not attending or resident in [land-grant] colleges in the several communities and imparting to such persons information on said subjects through field demonstrations, publications, and otherwise."[9]

Interestingly, if we look at Extension's national website today we find that Extension work is still described in remarkably similar ways. On that website, we find that Extension professionals' work involves "taking knowledge gained through research and education and bringing it directly to the people." We find that they "provide research-based information to its range of audiences" and "bring vital, practical information to agricultural producers, small business owners, consumers, families, and young people." And we find that Extension as an institution "provides non-formal education and learning activities" and "brings evidence-based science and modern technologies to farmers, consumers, and families."[10]

These are activities. They don't tell us anything about Extension's purposes. Interestingly, the Smith-Lever Act doesn't say anything at all about purpose. But Extension's contemporary national website does. There, Extension's purposes are described in the following phrases: "to create positive changes"; "to address public needs"; to contribute "to the success of countless farms, ranches, and rural businesses"; to "improve the lives of consumers and families"; "to address a wide range of human, plant, and animal needs in both urban and rural areas"; and "to improve agricultural, economic, and social conditions."[11]

It would take an entire book to explore the many conflicting ways these purposes have been viewed and pursued by Extension professionals. To make a long story short, the dominant view of Extension's main purpose, both today and during most of its history, is to address problems *in* democracy through the provision and application of scientific and technical knowledge and expertise. But here's where Extension becomes interesting. During its long history, many women and men articulated an aspirational vision of Extension's purposes and practices that connected work on problems *in* democracy with problems *of* democracy, in ways that were explicitly attentive to the cultivation of democratic practices. For example, in an article that was published in 1934 in Extension's national journal, the *Extension Service Review*, R. J. Baldwin, who served as director of Extension in Michigan for more than 30 years, proclaimed the following:

> The program of extension work in agriculture and home economics for 20 years has been based on the policy of personal participation on the part of farm people in the analysis of economic, social, and other problems, and in the carrying out of the solutions of them. Through these experiences they have discovered and developed their own capacities for learning and leadership. Studying, thinking and acting together has stimulated growth, nourished initiative and inspired self-dependence. Out of their achievements in farm, home, community, State, and national programs have come much

confidence, courage, and understanding. . . . This development
of people themselves, through their own efforts, I believe is the
Extension Service's most valuable contribution to society.[12]

It's important to note that what Baldwin is communicating here are
not "facts" about what actually happened in all, or even most, cases. We
would be naïve to see it that way. Rather, we should read this passage as an
aspirational vision of what he (and others) thought *should be* happening
in Extension work, and as a direct result, how we should understand the
larger significance of that work for the people who participate in it, and
for the nation as a whole.

At the same time, it's important to note that the vision Baldwin
communicates wasn't (and isn't) *merely* aspirational. It was actually opera-
tionalized in many ways and places—and is still today, as the stories in
this book's profiles reveal. The largest and boldest example we know of in
Extension history was launched in 1935, the year after Baldwin's article was
published. In that year, USDA established a Program Study and Discussion
(PSD) unit. Based on something called "the discussion method," over the
next five years PSD brought millions of rural women and men together in
tens of thousands of small groups to discuss a wide range of pressing public
issues and problems, and engage in deliberation about different alternatives
for addressing them. The groups were facilitated by more than 60,000 local
discussion leaders who were specifically trained for the task. And they were
organized by Extension professionals.[13] (See this book's final chapter for
a detailed account of this initiative.)

As with many other democratic efforts in American history, those who
led and organized this work in Extension were met with resistance—not
only from sources external to Extension, but also from within. Gladys Baker
reveals the latter in the following passage from her book, *The County Agent*,
which was published in 1939:

> County agents who were responsible for setting up the discussion
> groups in communities and counties were not always enthusias-
> tic about this additional project advocated by the Department
> of Agriculture at a time when they were already burdened with

numerous federal programs. The training and experience of the agents did not fit them with the necessary tolerance and objectivity for this task; for they were accustomed to parceling out a continuous supply of "right answers" to immediately pressing farm problems and consequently often found it difficult to see the practical value of philosophical discussion groups. Leaders in some states reported that it was difficult to keep the county agent from monopolizing the discussion and insisting that his viewpoint and judgment be accepted by the group.[14]

The resistance Baker illuminates here is partly a function of Extension's identity and culture as a development institution, and of the training of Extension staff as development professionals. As a development institution, Extension's work has long been focused on the improvement (i.e., "development") of places and people for reasons that are mainly material and economic in nature, in ways that are supposed to advance the interests and power of a nation-state (in this case, the United States). Professionals who are hired and trained to do "development" work in institutions like Extension often include as one of their practices something that the anthropologist and development scholar Tania Murray Li describes as "rendering technical." In short, the practice of rendering technical involves the work of simplifying complex situations and problems in ways that make them appear to be solvable—or at least improvable—through interventions that deploy and apply professionals' technical expertise and knowledge. As Li points out, the practice of rendering technical often incorporates a simultaneous practice that she calls "rendering nonpolitical." This practice, which is part of the "simplifying" process in development work, involves the exclusion or bracketing out of political structures, dynamics, and processes from the diagnoses and prescriptions that experts make of particular situations. It reflects a rejection of politics as a means of understanding and addressing problems, and an embrace instead of technical expertise.

All of this isn't necessarily a result of malicious intent on the part of development professionals. As Li argues, it's often subliminal and routine. "Experts are trained to frame problems in technical terms," Li writes. "This is their job. Their claim to expertise depends on their capacity to diagnose problems in ways that match the kinds of solution that fall within their repertoire."[15]

With the problems Baker and Li illuminate, we can begin to see why many critics have viewed Extension and the professionals it employs as an *anti*-democratic force in civic life.[16] And these critics are right. Extension has been such a force in the past. All too often, it still is today. But most critics miss an important truth. Throughout its existence, Extension has employed some professionals who have understood and pursued their work in ways that are aligned—imperfectly, of course—with the task of making democracy work as it should. Our favorite articulation of the vision behind this truth can be found in the following passage from Ruby Green Smith's history of Cornell University's Extension work, which was published in 1949 under the evocative title, *The People's Colleges*:

> Extension workers need to have faith in spiritual values and to recognize the human relationships that contribute to what the ancient Greeks called "the good life." They should believe that in the kind of homes, farms, and industries which are the goals of Extension service "man cannot live by bread alone"; that it is not enough for people to have food, shelter, and clothing—that they aspire also to find appreciation, respect for individuality and human dignity, affection, ideals, and opportunities. These are the satisfactions that belong to democratic living.[17]

WHY AND HOW WE COCREATED THE PROFILES IN THIS BOOK

As faculty members of land-grant universities who work on a regular basis with Extension professionals, we embrace Ruby Green Smith's vision. We see it as a call for Extension professionals to respectfully, humbly, and carefully jump into civic life, in ways that address problems *of* as well as *in* democracy, and help make democracy work as it should. One way we pursue our ongoing commitment to this vision and work is through the research that led to this book (and many other publications).[18] In our research, we have been looking for Extension professionals who share this commitment with us, even if they don't name it the way we do. We're happy to report that we have found hundreds of them. The reason why we cocreated the oral history profiles in this book is to make some of their stories available for others to learn from. We're convinced their stories offer many lessons and insights for professionals in a wide range of institutions.

We took several steps in our research to cocreate the oral history profiles in this book. First, we identified Extension professionals who we had reason to believe—either from personal experience or by reputation—were engaged as professionals in the task of making democracy work as it should (whether they thought of their work in that way or not). Second, working with Kettering senior associate Alice Diebel, we convened dozens of them in research exchanges at the Kettering Foundation, during which we invited them to share stories about their experiences and work. Third, we conducted individual narrative interviews with 25 of them.

We approached each of our interviews as open-ended conversations divided into three relatively equal parts. In the first part, we invited our interviewees to tell us where they grew up, what experiences and which people shaped them, and how they ended up as Extension professionals.[19] In the second part, we invited them to tell practice stories about specific public work projects they've been engaged in as Extension professionals. We asked them how they got involved in these projects, and encouraged them to tell stories about what happened. We wanted to hear stories that included all the elements of good storytelling: settings and scenes; characters; plots; conflict; actions and reactions; and resolutions or ending points. Finally, we asked them to interpret the meaning and significance of their experiences, and to name key lessons they draw from them.

All of the interviews we conducted were audio recorded and transcribed, word-for-word. Using a light hand, we then edited the transcripts into what we refer to as oral history profiles. We then picked eight of the profiles for inclusion in this book. We chose profiles that have instructive and provocative life and practice stories that our interviewees granted us permission to publish. We were not concerned about whether the profiles we selected would be "representative" of anything or anyone, such as the "average" Extension professional, or a full scope of diversity with respect to field, geography, gender, or race.

The eight profiles we include in this book are of five women and three men, from six different states: Alabama, Delaware, Indiana, Kansas, Michigan, and Oklahoma. We've already introduced them in the thumbnail sketches we provided earlier in this introduction. Now we want to provide readers with a set of three interrelated interpretive tools they can use to make sense of the stories professionals tell in their profiles.

INTERPRETING THE STORIES

It's of critical importance that readers understand that the profiles in this book are not essays or case studies. They are lightly edited oral histories. While they include professionals' opinions and views about many things, they also—and more important—include life stories in the form of biographies, and stories of their experiences and practices in their institutions, and in civic life as participants in public work. While stories are common, edited transcriptions of storytelling in the form we present them in this book are not. For many reasons, interpreting them is a difficult task, both intellectually and ethically.

Rebecca Solnit offers us an important truth to remember as we engage in the complex work of interpretation. "Where does a story begin?" she asks in her book, *The Faraway Nearby*. In her lyrical voice, she answers: "The fiction is that they do, and end, rather than that the stuff of story is just a cup of water scooped from the sea and poured back into it."[20] The truth we find in this passage invites us to approach the task of telling, listening to, and interpreting stories with reverence and humility. For what we tell, hear, and interpret are only fragments of an immense, teeming sea of ever-changing life that is beyond our abilities to fully know, in a world we all see and experience differently, whatever we may hold in common. No interpreter of a story, or of the person who tells it, should therefore seek definitive finality in their interpretations.[21] We should not, of course, allow that to hinder us from making provisional interpretations. But we need to be humble and reverent, clear about our purposes, and conscious of our limited subjective perspectives. We also need useful tools to employ.

As we have already stated, our purpose here is to help open our collective imagination to possibilities for professionals to jump into civic life in ways that support the task of making democracy work as it should. In pursuit of this purpose, we have already offered two interpretive tools: first, the idea that stories are a means for us to communicate and consider the "truths of our experiences," which storytellers offer us in the "truth of the telling," rather than (only) in the telling of the truth; and second, the brief background we provided about Extension, which we can use as a tool to situate the stories the professionals tell in their profiles. Now, we'd like to offer three more tools.

UNFINISHED SCRIPTS AND STORIES

The first of the three additional interpretive tools we offer emerges from two sentences in Arthur Frank's book, *Letting Stories Breathe*:

> People grow up being cast into stories, as actors are cast into their parts in a play—but that is too deterministic a metaphor. People are like actors cast into multiple scripts that are all unfinished.[22]

These sentences remind us that we live in a world that has been and is being scripted, storied, and re-storied in multiple, unfinished ways. They also remind us that we have all been cast into multiple scripts or stories in parts or roles that are not always of our own choosing. Finally, they suggest the hopeful possibility of agency: as actors who have been cast in multiple *unfinished* scripts, we can participate in writing and performing next scenes. And we can change the roles we play by re-storying the story or stories into which we've been cast.

One of Frank's sources of inspiration in writing these two sentences was the following passage from Alasdair MacIntyre's book, *After Virtue*:

> I can only answer the question "What am I to do?" if I can answer the prior question "Of what story or stories do I find myself a part?" We enter human society, that is, with one or more imputed characters—roles into which we have been drafted— and we have to learn what they are in order to be able to understand how others respond to us and how our responses to them are apt to be construed.[23]

The tool we're offering here can be used to illuminate what we have come to see as the most important move professionals can make in opening up possibilities for constructive contribution to the task of making democracy work as it should: *finding themselves as actors in multiple scripts and stories that are all unfinished, one of which relates to the ongoing task of making democracy work as it should*. While they don't explicitly name it, this is one of the things we find the professionals in this book doing in their life and practice stories. In reading their profiles, we encourage readers to use what we've written here as a tool not only to see what this move involves, in context and in action, but also to make sense of its significance and meaning.

THE LIVING RELATIONS OF PERSON TO PERSON

This brings us to our next tool. John Dewey once argued that "we have taken democracy for granted," forgetting that it "has to be enacted anew in every generation, in every year and day, in the living relations of person to person in all social forms and institutions."[24] We can use Dewey's argument as an interpretive tool to elevate our understanding of the significance of what we see the professionals doing in the stories they tell in this book. Using this tool, we can see that they are not just providing technical assistance or expertise. They are also *enacting democracy*, performing roles they are choosing to take up as they coauthor next scenes in their civic work. They are attending to problems *of* democracy, "in the living relations of person to person," in ways that are connected to and interwoven with their attention to problems *in* democracy. Most important for us, we learn from their life stories that their motivations for doing so are grounded in a particular way of understanding their identities and purposes—both as professionals employed by a particular institution, and as citizens.

At the heart of what's particular about their identities and purposes are the ways in which they are positioned *in* rather than *apart from* the public work of civic life. By positioning themselves this way, we can say that they are functioning as what theorists have called "civic professionals," "democratic professionals," or "citizen professionals."[25] Their stories bring these theoretical types to life, enhancing our understanding of the nature and meaning of the practices such professionals use in their work (as well as the purposes they pursue), what and who support them, and what and who stand in the way.

SITUATIONAL IMPROVISATIONS

Our final interpretive tool, related closely to the other two, is simply a recognition of what competent and publicly responsible professional practice involves. In short, it's rarely if ever the performance of "best practices," the scripted implementation of "evidence-based programs," or the mechanical application of scientific knowledge, models, ideas, or theories. Instead, it's chiefly a complex set of improvised moves and judgments, made in relation to readings of specific situations, and guided and shaped in selective ways by previous experience, conceptual frameworks, theories of change, political and economic realities (including various kinds of power), and institutional, personal, and collective identities, philosophies, ideals, interests, purposes, and commitments.

Far more than the mechanical performance of practice routines, what we see in the stories we read in this book are situational improvisations— spirited expressions of who these professionals are, what they stand for, and what they aim to advance in their lives and work. These are things that are not commonly revealed or discussed in many professional fields and institutions. They reveal hidden dimensions of practice that often go both unexamined and unnamed. And we see something else in these stories that is often left unexamined and unnamed: incomplete or ambiguous results, and struggles with counterforces emanating both from professionals' institutions and from the communities in which they work.

Of course, we all already knew that work in the real world is and must always be improvisational, and both incomplete and mixed in its results. One reason we state the obvious here is to push back against dystopian fantasies that are being propagated (once again) in institutions like Extension, often by well-meaning people. These fantasies, which are pursued through technocratic approaches to problem solving, can lead us to doubt our common

sense, our faith in democracy, and the value of telling and learning from stories. We must resist them. One way we have done so is by making this book.

CONCLUDING NOTE

Now (finally!) we invite readers to read the profiles in this book, using
the interpretive tools we have provided, as well as their own. But first, we
want to offer one more thing our readers may want to keep in mind.

We often turn to stories for instruction, hoping they might tell us what
we should do in relation to the choices we face in challenging situations.
For the kinds of situations we're interested in, that's problematic. While
good stories can be instructive, it would be misguided to expect them to
provide us with step-by-step instructions for our own lives and work. On
this point, listen to what Jan Hartough tells us in her profile:

important

> I would never tell somebody to say, "Oh, do it exactly this way."
> I think sometimes people are looking for that. "We're just going
> to do step one, two, and three." I really caution them because I
> think you might be able to use step three, but none of the other
> steps. Communities really need to talk about their situation. A
> lot of times they'd rather just take what they did over in this other
> community and just try to plop it into their community without
> allowing citizens to talk about what's happening. I think, yeah,
> there are a lot of parts that could be replicated in another com-
> munity. But I would caution that community to really talk about
> what it is they really want to do. That's why we're not saying
> there are models. We're working with situations. There are some
> results and impacts that came out of working with this situation.
> Perhaps some of these ideas you can use over here and then add
> to it or subtract or whatever. I think that's the way it needs to
> be presented.

Keeping this in mind, an important step we can take in our efforts
to make sense of the stories we hear is to add to them by telling our own
stories, live and in person, to each other. This isn't an exotic or academic
idea. It's something we already do quite naturally. We name it here to
reinforce one of our convictions: our learning about and from the profiles
in this book is best done with others, rather than alone. "The capacity of

stories," Arthur Frank says, "is to explore complications, rarely to resolve them."[26] And we explore stories' complications not just by using theoretical and conceptual tools and frameworks, but also by telling and listening to more stories.

We hope this book inspires a lot of storytelling, and with it, a desire for deeper listening and learning. Most important, we hope it strengthens readers' commitments to support opportunities for everyone to partake in the satisfactions of democratic living.

ENDNOTES

[1]   On the history, philosophy, and practice of public work, see Harry C. Boyte's work, especially in *Everyday Politics: Reconnecting Citizens and Public Life* (Philadelphia, PA: University of Pennsylvania Press, 2004), and *Awakening Democracy through Public Work: Pedagogies of Empowerment* (Nashville, TN: Vanderbilt University Press, 2018).

[2]   David Mathews, *The Ecology of Democracy: Finding Ways to Have a Stronger Hand in Shaping Our Future* (Dayton, OH: Kettering Foundation Press, 2014), 119-120.

[3]   On this theme, see John McKnight, *The Careless Society: Community and Its Counterfeits* (New York: Basic Books, 1995); and *The Four-Legged Stool*, a study published by the Kettering Foundation in 2013, available for free download at https://www.kettering.org/catalog/product/four-legged-stool.

[4]   Mathews, *The Ecology of Democracy*, xvii-xviii and 3-5.

[5]   Personal Narratives Group, *Interpreting Women's Lives: Feminist Theory and Personal Narratives* (Indiana University Press, 1989), 261.

[6]   See Kevin M. Bradt, *Story as a Way of Knowing* (Kansas City, MO: Sheed & Ward, 1997).

[7]   Alessandro Portelli, *The Battle of Vale Giulia: Oral History and the Art of Dialogue* (Madison, WI: University of Wisconsin Press, 1997), 48.

[8]   Budget and staffing data provided by the Cooperative Extension Measuring Excellence in Extension Implementation Team, Joe Zublena, Chair, North Carolina State University, November 20, 2013.

[9]   Smith-Lever Act, quoted from Alfred C. True, *A History of Agricultural Extension Work in the United States, 1785-1923* (Miscellaneous Publication No. 36. Washington, DC: United States Department of Agriculture, 1928), 195.

[10]   All quotations taken from https://nifa.usda.gov/extension, accessed June 9, 2016.

[11]   Ibid.

[12] R. J. Baldwin, "Outlook Broadened," *Extension Service Review* vol. 5 no. 6 (June 1934): 89, 95.

[13] On this initiative, which also included county land-use planning, see Jess Gilbert, *Planning Democracy: Agrarian Intellectuals and the Intended New Deal* (New Haven, CT: Yale University Press, 2015).

[14] Gladys Baker, *The County Agent* (Chicago, IL: University of Chicago Press, 1939), 85.

[15] Tania Murray Li, *The Will to Improve: Governmentality, Development, and the Practice of Politics* (Durham, NC: Duke University Press, 2007), 7. For more on the themes raised in this paragraph, see James Ferguson, *The Anti-Politics Machine: "Development," Depoliticization, and Bureaucratic Power in Lesotho* (Minneapolis, MN: University of Minnesota Press, 1994); and James C. Scott, *Seeing Like a State: How Certain Schemes to Improve the Human Condition Have Failed* (Yale University Press, 1999).

[16] Among the many, many works by critics who have accused Extension or land-grant institutions of being antidemocratic, see especially Jim Hightower, *Hard Tomatoes, Hard Times* (Cambridge, MA: Schenkman Publishing Company, 1973, 1978); Wendell Berry, *The Unsettling of America: Culture and Agriculture, 3rd edition* (San Francisco, CA: Sierra Club Books, 1977, 1996); Gordon Gary Scoville, *Anti-Democracy's College: An Outline of the Corporatist Culture of Organized Social Machinery and the Leadership of the Land-Grant Agricultural Colleges in the "Progressive" Era* (Unpublished doctoral dissertation, Montana State University, 1990); Frieda Knobloch, *The Culture of Wilderness: Agriculture as Colonization in the American West* (Chapel Hill: University of North Carolina Press, 1996); Deborah Fitzgerald, *Every Farm a Factory: The Industrial Ideal in American Agriculture* (New Haven, CT: Yale University Press, 2003); Christopher R. Henke, *Cultivating Science, Harvesting Power: Science and Industrial Agriculture in California, 2nd edition* (Cambridge, MA; MIT Press, 2008); and Gabriel N. Rosenberg, *The 4-H Harvest: Sexuality and the State in Rural America* (Philadelphia, PA: University of Pennsylvania Press, 2016).

[17] Ruby Green Smith, *The People's Colleges* (Ithaca, NY: Cornell University Press, 1949), 544. Cornell University Press republished this book in 2013, with a new preface by Scott J. Peters, "The Pursuit of Happiness, Public and Private."

[18] Publications from our previous work include Scott J. Peters, Nicholas R. Jordan, Margaret Adamek, and Theodore R. Alter (eds.), *Engaging Campus and Community: The Practice of Public Scholarship in the State and Land-Grant University System* (Dayton: Kettering Foundation Press, 2005); Scott J. Peters, "Every Farmer Should Be Awakened: Liberty Hyde Bailey's Vision of Agricultural Extension Work," *Agricultural History*, vol. 80, no. 2 (Spring 2006): 190-219; Scott J. Peters, Daniel J. O'Connell, Theodore R. Alter, and Allison Jack (eds.), *Catalyzing Change: Profiles of Cornell Cooperative Extension Educators from Greene, Tompkins, and Erie Counties, New York* (Ithaca, NY: Cornell Cooperative Extension, 2006); Scott J. Peters, "Reconstructing a Democratic Tradition of Public Scholarship in the Land-Grant System," in *Agent of Democracy: Higher Education and the HEX Journey*, edited by D. Brown, and D. Witte (Dayton, OH: Kettering Foundation Press, 2008), 121-148; Scott J. Peters, Theodore R. Alter, and Neil Schwartzbach, "Unsettling a Settled Discourse: Faculty Views of the Meaning and Significance of the Land-Grant Mission," *Journal of Higher Education Outreach and Engagement*, vol. 12(2) (2008): 33-66; Scott J. Peters, Theodore R. Alter,

and Neil Schwartzbach, *Democracy and Higher Education: Traditions and Stories of Civic Engagement* (East Lansing: Michigan State University Press, 2010); Jeffrey C. Bridger and Theodore R. Alter, "Public Sociology, Public Scholarship, and Community Development," *Community Development*, vol. 41:4 (2010): 405-416; Jeffrey C. Bridger and Theodore R. Alter, "The Engaged University, Community Development, and Public Scholarship," *Journal of Higher Education Outreach and Engagement*, vol. 11(1) (2011): 163-178; Scott J. Peters, "Storying and Restorying the Land-Grant Mission," in *The Land-Grant Colleges and the Reshaping of American Higher Education, Perspectives on the History of Higher Education*, vol. 30, edited by Roger L. Geiger and Nathan M. Sorber (New Brunswick, NJ: Transaction Publishers, 2013), 335-353; and Timothy J. Shaffer, "What Should You and I Do? Lessons for Civic Studies from Deliberative Politics in the New Deal," *The Good Society*, 22(2) (2013): 137-150.

[19]   Our attentiveness approach to drawing out "practice stories" is inspired by John Forester's work. See especially John Forester, *The Deliberative Practitioner: Encouraging Participatory Planning Processes* (Cambridge, MA: MIT Press, 1999); John Forester, *Dealing with Differences: Dramas of Mediating Public Disputes* (New York: Oxford University Press, 2009); and Ken Reardon and John Forester (eds.), *Rebuilding Community after Katrina: Transformative Education in the New Orleans Planning Initiative* (Philadelphia, PA: Temple University Press, 2016).

[20]   Rebecca Solnit, *The Faraway Nearby* (New York: Penguin Books, 2013), 27.

[21]   This is the theme of Arthur W. Frank's book, *Letting Stories Breathe: A Socio-Narratology* (Chicago, IL: University of Chicago Press, 2010), which centers on what he calls dialogical narrative analysis.

[22]   Arthur Frank, *Letting Stories Breathe*, 7.

[23]   Alasdair MacIntyre, *After Virtue: A Study in Moral Theory* (Notre Dame: University of Notre Dame Press, 1981/1984), 216.

[24]   John Dewey, "Education and Social Change," *Social Frontier 3* (May 1937): 237.

[25]   On the idea of "civic professionals," see William Sullivan, *Work and Integrity: The Crisis and Promise of Professionalism in America* (San Francisco, CA: Jossey-Bass, 2005). On "democratic professionals," see Albert W. Dzur, *Democratic Professionalism: Citizen Participation and the Reconstruction of Professional Ethics, Identity, and Practice* (University Park, PA: The Pennsylvania State University Press, 2008). On "citizen professionals," see Harry C. Boyte, *Reinventing Citizenship as Public Work: Citizen-Centered Democracy and the Empowerment Gap* (Dayton, OH: Kettering Foundation, 2013, available online at https://www.kettering.org/catalog/product/reinventing-citizenship-public-work-citizen-centered-democracy-and-empowerment-gap-0). For a recent exploration of civic professionalism in higher education, see Novella Zett Keith, *Engaging in Social Partnerships: Democratic Practices for Campus-Community Partnerships* (New York: Routledge, 2015).

[26] Arthur Frank, *Letting Stories Breathe*.

How About We Get Together?

A Profile of Carmen DeRusha
Extension Educator, Economic & Community Development
Purdue University

How can people come together to build the kind of community they want? David Mathews has written that this is every community's question, regardless of its location and circumstances. In this profile, Carmen DeRusha not only shows us how she has sought to align her practices and routines as an Extension professional with people who want to take up this question, but also why. "How" involves the many dimensions of strategic, long-term, and highly relational leadership development and organizing work. "Why" flows from anger about injustices, apathy, and disconnected institutions, which has roots in her childhood in Colombia. It involves a passion for public work, which is also rooted in her childhood experiences, and a fierce commitment to the expansion of opportunities for people to learn and grow through their own engagement in the process.

My name is Carmen DeRusha and I have been with Extension for 19 years. My journey to Extension began as I developed a passion for social justice as a child. I was born in a very small town in the central part of Colombia, South America, in a region called Boyacá. The town where I was born is called San Mateo.

I am the second of a family of seven children: three girls and four boys. My parents were very young when they decided to have a family. My mother was 18 when she became a mom and my dad was 22. They had all these children very quickly. My dad is a teacher, but initially he was going to be a priest. He was very educated in theology, philosophy, Greek and Latin, and all those kinds of things. Then suddenly he changed careers, and rather than become a father for the Church, he became a father for a very large family. He was very young and so was my mother.

After living in San Mateo for some time near my father's family, we moved to live close to my mother's family, which was in another small town. At the age of 11, we moved to a medium-sized city, which is called Tunja, where I probably spent the most time in my life. This city is particularly interesting. It is about 470 years old. It was a very important religious settlement during colonial times, has a lot of beautiful churches, is very colonial looking, and has seven universities. So that is the kind of place people look to when they want to study and do better. My father was a teacher by profession. My mother was also a teacher—an elementary school teacher—but she stopped working when she had her fourth child.

I can clearly remember being at the age of 13 years old with people who were teenagers like me, and we did not have a lot of things to do. We did not have television in my home. We got television when I was 14 years old. Maybe we could not afford it, or maybe it was not that interesting, because we did not have a color TV for years. So we were kind of always thinking, "What are we going to do?" Someone, I do not know who, had the idea, "Let's go and paint this school." So we found paint and everybody went and painted the school. This school was dirty. After we finished painting it, it was such an amazing feeling. The pride! We did it! We painted the school. After that it was very natural for me to become involved in what was going on.

The place that we lived in was a working-class neighborhood. We did not have a lot of resources, but we had enough. We had a "comfortable life." But moving from a small town to another small town to a medium-sized town, I just witnessed an amazing disconnect between the institutions and what I saw around me. The poverty of most people was staggering. Riding on those roads and looking at the poverty, the hard work, and the despair, and what violence had done for people and all of that—I was just unhappy about all of those things, naturally. Since the time that I was conscious about who I was, I have been very unhappy about those situations.

So, as I said, when I was 13 I had my first opportunity to do something, which was paint that public school. I did it and I felt fabulous. That became part of my life—that experience of doing something, improving something that I did not like. I recognized that the world was not a nice place for everybody. But it could be a nice place, so I became passionate about making the world a better place.

My dad is very religious. But I just could not see the connection between religion and its impact on people. There were these people living in these beautiful places, and then all these children without families—hungry, roaming the streets and sniffing glue, and stealing to be able to survive. Everybody was just like, "This is not our problem." Not even religion or education! It was a lot of unhappiness.

At the time of this unhappiness, it was time for me to go into high school. I elected to get a degree as a teacher. You could do that at that time in Colombia. My school was called a *normales*, or normal school.

When I began my career as a teacher, I knew that there were so many kids who were in difficult situations. I thought, "The school can't fix that. We have to work with the parents." So we created programs to work with the parents. I created pedagogical sessions, where we organized conversations about how we could provide better education to these kids, because we are it; we teachers are it for them. I realized that some teachers did not have that conscience. I worked a lot with that, and the principal allowed me to do those things.

I changed some of the systems in the school. Rather than favoring the best kids, we favored the kids who made progress. We changed the pyramid. We had to support the kids who did not have confidence, because they are the ones we cannot lose. (By the way, that's why I wish we could modify Extension's 4-H slogan: "Making the best better." We should strive to "make everyone better," with an emphasis on youth with fewer opportunities.)

Following these principles, I changed a lot of things. I replaced the end-of-the-year staff celebration with a carnival for everyone. In three years, I changed so many things. My parents and my siblings were my volunteers. They still remember, to this day, feeling like, "Please don't look for any more projects for us!" They were always my resource to do things. We didn't have money, and so . . .

While I was a teacher I met a man from Wisconsin, who later became my husband. Before I entered college, I studied music a little bit, because I like music. I befriended a lot of musicians in town. For that reason, when I got out of college and my friends were working at the school of music, they asked me to help them with a specific project. My school lent me for one year to the music school to do a project there. I put a general curriculum together with the music curriculum so the younger kids could become good instrumentalists, and they would not have to work extra every day. It was there I met my husband, who was a musician working at the school of music.

Falling in love was the most ridiculous thing. It was not rational. It did not make any sense. It was not in my plans. It was just something that happened. I guess what I learned about life, and more about love, is that you do not look for it. You do not have a checklist. It just happens. So it happened to me, and it derailed my whole career in Colombia. At the time I had been accepted to a master's program there. I found the perfect master's program, which was to do education and social development. So that is my master's. It was perfect, the two things I was interested in.

I finished my master's, and after a five-year relationship with my husband, we decided to get married. He is a classical musician, so there were not very many opportunities in Colombia for him. I was young and the opportunity to leave and get to know other things was kind of alluring to me. I said, "Why not? Sure. Let's do it." We got married. In the back of my mind I thought, "Maybe this is not going to work, but we will try it. Why not?" So we moved to the United States in 1986. I came without the language. I did not know how to speak English. I had never studied

English, because I went to a normal-curriculum school in Colombia, so we did not have a second language. The little I learned in college was not enough.

I came here and I cried for about six months because I could not talk to anybody. I had a master's degree and I could not talk to anybody. I did not know how to. It was very traumatic. Then, after that I said, "No, I can do it." I looked in the paper for a job. I found a job with a non-profit organization called La Casa de Puerto Rico, located in Hartford, Connecticut. My husband was a professor at Hartt School of Music. I went to work in inner-city Hartford.

At the time, Hartford was the fourth poorest city in the country, in the richest state of the union. It was again just this disconnect. So I said, "Hey, this is not only happening in Colombia! It happens everywhere! So I can do social justice, improve the world anywhere I go!" I had the opportunity to meet a lot of people in different positions through my husband's job. And then I did my job, so I had a comprehension of the disparity in the United States—the disparity of class and opportunities. I had that critical mind that was very helpful to see where I was. I found that I could do this kind of job here, even in the most industrialized and richest country. There were always opportunities to work on social justice issues.

In my master's studies I learned about ethnography as a tool for doing research. I became acquainted with experiential action research. That was my training. In terms of curriculum, my master's is equivalent to a PhD here. We did a lot of research. We went through a lot of the social science research. There were not a lot of people with my level of education working at La Casa de Puerto Rico. My English was not very good, but I was a very good employee. They really liked me and they soon promoted me. After three years, I was the director of a statewide project called Family Resource Centers that was approved by the legislature in Connecticut. It was a great learning experience. Then I was recruited by the Institute for Community Research in Hartford, Connecticut. I worked for them for three years. I learned a lot and my English became much better.

After that, my husband found a job in Indianapolis and we moved. We got to Indianapolis and I told my husband, "It's your fault that we are here. I don't have a job. I'm going to take four or six months just to get to know the area. I don't want to do anything." But after I sat in the house for three weeks, I was just like, "What am I going to do?"

I made a list of institutions that I could volunteer at. One of my friends who was a musician and worked at a university said, "You know what? There are Extension offices here. They work with a lot of migrant workers, and they speak Spanish. Maybe they want you to volunteer." I called the Extension office, one of the places I was going to volunteer, and I told the receptionist, "I am looking for a volunteer opportunity. I just moved into the city." She said, "Well, do you have a master's degree?" I said, "Yes, I have a master's degree." Then the receptionist said, "Well, we have three job openings." I said, "No, Mary. I'm not really looking for a job. I want to volunteer and explore a little bit more." Mary said, "Well, why don't you come and just take a look at what we have?" This is the receptionist, who later on became my secretary. We had a great relationship.

I went there and I brought my résumé. Ned Kalb, the county Extension director, looked at my résumé and said, "We really would like you to work for us." I said, "Okay, what do I need to do?" He said, "There are three job descriptions." There was a Consumer and Family Sciences (CFS) opportunity, there was a 4-H opening, and there was something that they called a special project coordinator. The special project coordinator position had a paragraph description that said, "We would like you to bring Extension to nontraditional audiences." I liked that one. It fit my profile. I had never had a job that had a job description, except when I was in the school system. It sounded fun.

The Far East Side Project

So I began my Extension career in 1991. My assignment was to bring Purdue Extension services to new audiences. Of course, when I learned more about the organization, I understood what they meant by it. "New audiences" meant people of color and poor people. They did not say that, but I understood that is what they meant.

Then I thought, "Okay, what am I going to do?" When you move to places, you develop a system for how you do things. The first thing: meet people. I began meeting people and learning about the city. I discovered that there was a place that everybody talked about, which was a neighborhood on the Far East Side. It was this troubled corner in the city—a very interesting corner, but it was abandoned. Basically, nobody paid attention to it. It was a dangerous place. There were no services. There were 5,000 kids with no access to recreational facilities, and all those kinds of things. I said, "Oh, maybe I have to check it out." So I went there and I began organizing individuals and organizations. I became the Far East Side representative, in a way.

I have learned that neighborhoods in urban areas are not communities. They are a collection of individuals who are struggling to survive. The Far East Side community was very challenged because Indianapolis has an approach to neighborhood development that emphasizes the neighborhoods next to downtown. Indianapolis, as a city, invested heavily in downtown. Now, every effort of community and neighborhood development around the downtown area receives a lot of attention and a lot of funding. But this neighborhood that I am talking about was on the outskirts of the city. At the time, it was called a suburban neighborhood with urban characteristics. So the same challenges that downtown had, this neighborhood had.

I went there because if there is no funding, people do not do anything. Being a part of Extension gave me the freedom to go and work there because we do have a very solid position, meaning we do not work with grants; we are employed year after year. So you can have the luxury of having a project that can take seven years, and really have an impact. I was not competing with anyone for grants. Agencies did not look at me as a threat, because I was not competing for any money that they had. Besides, none of them really wanted to do what I was doing. Organizing, as I understood it, was something that people were not comfortable doing, while I was comfortable, because it was my only choice. How do you go to a place where there is no community development (CD) infrastructure to work with? You have to create the CD infrastructure. To create it, you have to knock on doors, approach people individually, and recruit them.

It took me three years, from the first time I stepped into the Far East Side neighborhood, to create several committees, including the big one that was called the Far East Side Community Development Council. I recruited people and formed a council of about 40 people. That council was the payoff from a lot of work that I did with organizations, businesses, residents, apartment managers, child-care centers, police departments, and health-care centers.

This was my first project and it was the most challenging of all because I was new to the system, new to the city. They wanted something new to be done. I had to use not only what I knew about the issues of human development and social justice and social change, but I had to use all of who and what I was for this project.

That project lasted seven years. That was the frame. What I also would like to share with you is some of the main threads that run through all four of the projects I have worked on in Extension, all the things that I have known and experienced every time I encountered a project. My work with the Far East Side shows a lot of the threads that I experienced throughout my years in Extension.

When I went into the neighborhood, knocking on people's doors, my strategy was to go to organizations first. So I went to organizations and I told them, "This neighborhood is known for being in very bad shape. I have been told that you have 5,000 children that live in this neighborhood, and you do not have any recreational facilities, and you do not have any opportunities for these kids. And the crime is very high. I have been told that you do not know the jurisdiction of the police department. You do not know which fire department to call because there are three different fire departments here." And they said, "Yes, yes, we know all that. But we don't know what to do." I said, "Okay, how about we get together?" So that was the thing. "How about we get together? When are we getting together?"

So we began meeting. I am talking about three years of grassroots work. After three years, everybody began identifying me with the Far East Side, because of how I always introduced myself—"I work for Purdue Extension, but I am doing neighborhood development in the Far East Side." As we met, a lot of the foundations and a lot of the people began realizing that there was something happening in this neighborhood. Everybody wanted something to happen, so they got onboard.

Then I was approached by the Central Indiana Community Foundation. They said, "The Pew Charitable Trust has an RFP for this kind of neighborhood. It has to be suburban. And as you know, in Indianapolis, we do not have any programs for suburban areas because we focus a lot on the center township and the downtown area. Tell us what you have been doing and see if we can fund that. Let's apply for a grant."

We got together. Only foundations were welcome to apply for the grant. The Central Indiana Community Foundation and I partnered, and I have kept all archives of every single meeting. I took notes. I did minutes. I have agendas. I have it all documented. There was not any question about civic engagement, because everybody who came to the meetings had to sign on. I also had meetings when I went to apartment complexes.

This took three years of grassroots work, and a fourth year to prepare the proposal to the Pew Charitable Trust. We presented the proposal, and they accepted it. We were assigned one of eight grants in the nation. It was for $600,000. Then the Central Indiana Community Foundation and the Lilly Endowment put together another $400,000. That provided us with a million dollars! After that, I was just feeling out of place, because it was not my project anymore. I thought, "Wow, this is happening. Now these people are going to have staff and resources. Now the Apartment Managers' Council will have somebody that will help them facilitate and talk about all these issues."

The first two years after receiving the money was devoted to planning. This neighborhood has 33,000 people, so it is a very large neighborhood. With these resources from the Pew Charitable Trust and their coaching, based on what they were asking us to do, we increased the citizens' participation and the neighborhood participation. There were several neighborhoods involved. It wasn't only one neighborhood.

We did a full-blown neighborhood development project. We engaged the city. The city planners came. That was for six years. The last year of the work was the beginning of the implementation. We merged the Far East Side Community Development Council and everything that we could merge into one group called the Community Alliance for the Far East Side.

So 16 years after getting that money, the organization has 12 full-time people. It is a community development corporation. It is very well-respected and has its own building. A lot of the by-laws were written with residents' participation. So the neighborhood has an infrastructure that is working for them.

Reflections

What I learned from this work is that a lot of people in neighborhoods in urban areas fear each other. They are not communities. They do not know how to begin developing relationships, because there are no spaces— natural spaces—for that to be created. I think one of the things that I provided was opportunity for interaction. After that interaction happened, people created relationships. If you get people together more and more, you may be able to build trusting relationships, which is the glue that holds people together, and the keystone of building a community. I do not think relationship building is the only necessary element. But what I have learned is that it's indispensable for successful community development work.

The other thing that I think happens is that after you bring people together and you facilitate conversations, you begin teaching them skills. In the teaching of the skills, you can teach theory. You can provide workshops. But I think the most important thing is you as a role model.

For example, when I am facilitating a meeting, I have to tell the group, "Okay, I am facilitating, but I am not going to do this all my life. Let me tell you what it is that I am doing." I make them pay attention to what I am doing, and tell them that I have done other kinds of projects in a similar way. I know that my modeling has served me well because it obligates me to walk the talk. Otherwise people do not follow you or people do not pay attention. You cannot influence people if you do not walk the talk.

I also discovered that people in difficult circumstances unconsciously believe that there is something wrong with them. They think that they are in the position they are in because they are not good enough. Until I help them see that the problem is because they cannot see the rest of the world as I can see it through my education and through my experience, they really believe that they are lesser beings. That creates hopelessness.

One of my jobs is to help them recognize their gifts, and recognize that there is a system in place that put them where they are. It is not their fault, especially if they are in a generational cycle of poverty. So that really helps them to feel that they are capable of finding solutions. Our job is to give them the skills and to provide them with the opportunity and possibility to solve their own problems. You cannot do that if you feel inadequate, or if you feel guilty about who you are. You have to address that. That is an art in itself, I think. I do not know if I am doing it sometimes intuitively now with more experience, but just listening has been very powerful. People have come to me and said, "Finally I understand why I am in the situation I am in, and why my family has been in this situation, and has been for generations and generations in this neighborhood." So that really helps.

About Extension's 4-H slogan, "Making the Best Better," the problem is that it does not fly in an urban context. It is embarrassing, to tell you the truth. I have been embarrassed a lot by our inability to be at the cutting-edge of urban issues. The problem is even after 19 years of working for Extension, people cannot understand that I work for Extension. Everybody in the city believes that I work for IUPUI (Indiana University—Purdue University Indianapolis). "Are you with IUPUI?" "No. I am with

Purdue Extension." "Isn't Purdue Extension agriculture?" The barrier of image is so amazing for us that even after 19 years of work, people still affiliate me with this rural image that Extension has. Little by little that's changing, because 19 years is 19 years. But that rural image is very strong.

My Extension job requires building trust among those in the community. But I have to gain trust in me as well because, without trust, you cannot get very much done with anyone. I will tell you, I spend a lot of time just going to people's homes, knocking on doors. We meet at people's houses. I talk to the kids. We organized a block party and I went to help them cook, and I helped them organize. I spend a lot of time with them so they get to see me as one of them, not as the person that comes from the university to do a job. I need to show that I am, as they are, invested in improving their community.

I have friends here, now, and one of them says, "You know, you are like my sister." And I say, "Yes. You know, it is my privilege to be your sister. It is so nice." And again, I will tell them, "The only difference between you and me is that I am being paid to learn a lot about the things that you may need to fix your neighborhood. So use me. Ask me. What do you need?" Last time we met, we went through a list of things that they wanted me to help them with. That is the other thing: I have made a contract with them, which is that I am going to be here as long as I am useful. Useful means that I can support them in locating resources to help their communities. But it is not up to me to make decisions about their needs or their vision for their community.

Another example of the importance of building trust is the story of a young female neighborhood leader. She and I developed a personal relationship. We go out for lunch; I bring her books and she reads them. She sends me e-mails about what she reads. I am not giving her a class; I am just sharing what I know and what I think, with the hope that she will better understand her circumstances and her community, and visualize the possibilities. I can tell that she is going to be a community leader. I mean, she is already. She is young. She is a single mother. She has been in the neighborhood. She has lived in generational poverty. Her husband is in prison right now. I am not interacting with her as the master's degree professional from Purdue University to teach her a class about how she should live, because that is not going to do any good. I mean, she would just laugh at me, like, "Oh, yes. Sure." Our relationship is personal as well as professional. In this way, she is open to hearing my message. And she is flourishing!

I think one of the challenges that I have as being a part of Extension is I that believe in the mission of Extension, and I am totally sold on it. I discovered that my job is not to work for Purdue University; my job is to make Purdue University work for the people in communities because Purdue is a public university. Extension involves government, university, and community, but all three of them should work for the public. If I was working for a private institution, this approach would be problematic. My job is to work for the people in communities. So it makes me feel very comfortable working for that public institution, because I feel that I own it. It is not the president. It is not the dean. No. I own it. I have investments in that institution, and my job is to make the institution work for the public. So I feel extremely comfortable, and I feel that I have autonomy.

One of the biggest challenges I have encountered, because my job is in an urban area, is that a lot of the Extension programs are rooted in the School of Agriculture. In the School of Agriculture, technology is the most appreciated method to solve problems. But I believe that our current problems cannot be solved by technology. I really believe that we have enough technology to keep us safe if use it correctly. Where I see a great deficiency is in the human element. We need more work with people to create a core of universal principles that will allow us to be together, to work together, to care for each other. That cannot be done only with technology.

I think it is necessary to construct a cohesive identity about what we do and to be very clear and consistent in expressing the public value of what we do. That is part of what will bring my job meaning. Before I created that cohesive identity, I read two books. I read *Fifty Years of Extension* (a history of Purdue University Extension, written by Dave Thompson), because I did not know anything about Extension. The other book was about 4-H in Indiana. After I read those two books I started understanding what Extension was and how I could transfer it into an urban setting. This was very important for me to do, because I could not have the energy to do this work that is so demanding if I did not truly believe in what the organization is about, and what people need. So for me, now those two things are crystal clear.

My work in community development in an urban area has been challenging, as this was a unique position within the Extension system in Indiana. I felt throughout the years that I did not belong to the traditional Extension system. I was very close to leaving. I asked for a leave of absence for three years. I was doing community development work in the Latino community. I was creating the civic infrastructure in the Latino community, and I became the executive director of a couple of organizations. I helped merge four organizations and created one. I understood that my role as an Extension educator was not compatible with the need in the community for a qualified executive director. I did this work until the new organizations was on a solid footing, and then went back to continue my work as an Extension educator.

Those three years away from Extension helped me better understand my role and better understand some of the difficulties of urban work in Extension. I realized that my work was unique and different, and that my approach to the difficulties was to show the positive impact Extension in urban areas was making and to continue to bring attention to the fact that the population in the State of Indiana was largely becoming urban. Purdue Extension needed to capitalize on this demographic change to remain a relevant organization.

My work throughout the years has been very appreciated by the local communities, but not so much within the Purdue Extension system. I am certain that this situation will change, but for now it is difficult to be one the few lonely voices bringing up the need to bring Extension to urban areas. Developing a sense of belonging in Purdue Extension has been a long and sometimes difficult process. The story I tell myself is that there are many factors influencing my outsider's feeling. For one, I am an immigrant and a woman of color. I work only in urban areas, in community development. That's a unique profile for an Extension educator in Indiana.

As we talk about my experiences in Extension, several issues of democracy and participation emerge when I am out in communities and I struggle with them. One is the polarized discourse. This polarization is not based on research-based information, but on preconceived notions and ideas that people are mostly very passionate about, and they do not even know why. There is just polarization and no desire for the dialogue that is, in my opinion, absolutely basic for democracy.

Polarization has been a really bad problem in Indianapolis. After being there for 19 years, I have seen four different mayors: Republican, Democrat, Democrat, and Republican. What happens is you have to work with everybody. But if the Democrats know that I have worked with the Republicans, they do not invite me to be part of the new administration. Or if the Republicans saw me working with the Democrats, they do not invite me to the new group. It is not something I do wrong. It is just the essence of people looking at you as taking sides. Community development work helps you become acquainted with local politics. It is very difficult to remain neutral, but in community work we have to avoid getting entangled in partisan politics.

Besides partisan polarization, the other obstacle I see in communities is the lack of opportunity for conversation. This is a cultural difference between my Colombian upbringing and the United States. People tell you, "You never talk about politics. You never talk about money. You never talk about religion." When I came to the States, I asked, "So, what do people talk about!" We really just talk about the weather, and it becomes a very boring kind of interaction.

People in power use the mass media outlets as a way to manipulate opinion—not as a way to communicate knowledge or information, but as a way to manipulate. For example, the radio talk shows; you listen to them and you say, "You've got to be kidding. Do people really believe in what they are saying?" And they do! Then you read the statistics that say so-and-so has 25 million people listening, and you say, "What?" Then you listen to them and they have no problem lying.

Another thing is that people are busy and they do not see participation in community life as a priority. They think that no matter what they do, they are not going to affect anything. There is a sense of hopelessness out there. Like, "Oh, come on. Don't waste my time. They're going to do whatever they want to do and that is all." This type of thing I find in communities, and it worries me. It is very worrisome. It requires us to learn how to build confidence that people working together can make a difference.

Another incredibly important issue is the influence of money in our political process. We have a representative democracy. People need to elect someone who will actually represent them. Candidates need money to be elected, and only people with discretionary income can make contributions. It seems that only people with money can help elect the candidates that will represent their interests. In comparison, Extension educators spend their time in community-driven projects and objectives. That is where probably our relevance is, because if we are out there competing for the same money that everybody else is competing for, we will be competing to do the same things that everybody else does. Those are not necessarily the things that need to be done. Extension plays a role in communities that is not dependent on fluctuating funding or changing political parties.

A lot of the things that we need to do in communities are things for which, more often than not, money is not available. So we have the luxury of doing it, and it is very much needed. We have the luxury in Extension to do what is needed in communities with or without money for it, and to keep doing it as long as it is needed. I think that it is a luxury for me to be part of Extension. Now, if they did not have that platform, many of the things I have accomplished would not have been possible—*period*.

One of the things that was so amazing to me—it was like destiny, in a way—is that I have always been interested in education as a way of achieving social justice and pursuing social change. Then I found an organization that was defined as an institution whose mission was to bring education into communities to improve people's lives. That is my interpretation of what Extension is, and I have been operating with that compass. I had never heard of an organization with such a compelling mission before in my entire life.

To encounter this system, for me, was just like, "You've got to be kidding. Who created this thing?" So I went through reading a lot of books about Extension history and all of that. Then I understood the incredible roots that the organization had everywhere in the country, and in Indiana more than anything. When I talked to my husband and I told him about this job, he said, "You are going to work for one of the oldest organizations and probably one of the most important organizations, in Indiana." So that is kind of interesting.

I have to tell you that I have been with Extension for 19 years, and in 19 years I have only done four community development projects. The first one took seven years. The second one took three years. The third one took seven years. And the last one in which I have been involved is taking two years. The challenge now is that the second group that I worked with is coming back to ask for my help again. After you are in a community, you learn so much about the players and you learn so much about the people that it gets, in a way, easier. So some people tell other people, and it is easier to gain the trust of a community.

I mentioned that for me, it is just a great privilege to be involved with Extension because I began being part of the system and believing in the mission of the system. I was lucky enough to be given a job concept, not a job description. So I created my own identity. Let's put it that way. My identity was created based on the mission of the organization, not based on the methods or the structure of the system. But I have been becoming more comfortable with it. I believe that we need to construct, in anything that we do, a cohesive identity. The clarity of what are we doing and why we are doing it is important, especially in the work with the community.

For example, I will tell you about another project that I am involved in, which is called Multi-Ethnic Indiana. It is the only organization right now that exists in the state of Indiana where multiple ethnic groups come together to talk about issues. Extension has facilitated that forum for four years. It is statewide. We have organized one conference and we are on our way to organize the second. Right now, the Humanities Council, the Indiana History Center, and other organizations are contributing to the project. The same thing that happened in the Far East Side is happening in this organization: we are bringing people together to address cutting-edge issues independently of the availability of resources. We have the opportunity to be facilitators and innovators.

This is another example of where some people will ask, "What is Extension doing facilitating a multi-ethnic conference?" Well, the answer is very clear. We have become an increasingly diverse state. We need to make efforts to reach out to diverse communities and bring everybody into the conversation. Within the conversation, we will come up with ideas and solutions. The mission of this committee focuses on how we can make Indiana a more welcoming place for diverse ethnic groups. That is our mission. What a beautiful mission!

I wrestle a lot with the question of how we can get people who are different to engage. How do you engage people who are sidelined or marginalized citizens, people who are not making—or not allowed to make—decisions to a place where we can come together to create something better? I am convinced that Extension is the perfect model to improve communities if we make sure to focus on human development, because we need to build better human beings and improve education and work towards acquiring social justice. In the end, that's why and how I came to this work, and what I care about.

I am totally sold on Extension's mission. The Extension mission is to bring education to communities to improve the quality of their lives. That is Extension to me. That is the mission of Extension. I define education as bringing usable knowledge. The thing is, we have found that science is not the last word. I cannot say that research-based is the ultimate perfect knowledge. No. I want to bring usable knowledge, meaning that people can understand and can use it to improve their lives.

I believe in education as the way to empower individuals and communities, and I apply this principle to myself. I am consistently looking for personal and professional development opportunities. As communities become more diverse I need to learn more about diversity and inclusion. I have taken extensive training to become a diversity practitioner from an organization using a human development model. This knowledge has profoundly affected my understanding of people and communities.

Looking back on my job and life experiences, I notice that I have been consistent through all my life in working for social justice, improving communities to offer better opportunities to all. I realize that no matter what kind of job I have, I will always be pursuing this ultimate goal. With this issue of social justice, education is the most powerful tool. You can use it in any context: the context of the school, the context of the community, the context of the church. Whatever the context is, you can really work towards social justice using education. This is the reason why Extension is the organization that perfectly aligns with my personal values.

Interview conducted by Scott J. Peters and Theodore R. Alter

The Highest Form of Education

A Profile of Janet Ayres
Professor (Ret.), Department of Agricultural Economics
Purdue University

What do people who live in a small Indiana township need in order to influence and shape their collective future? In this profile, Janet Ayres shows us what it can look like when the answer is education—understood not as one-way transfers of expertise and information from universities to communities but rather as deliberative discourse that moves conversations from "I, mine, and me" to "we." Deliberative discourse engages people with different values and political views in listening as well as speaking; when it's working it makes them uncomfortable and produces "butterflies in the tummy and sweaty armpits." Janet facilitates these exchanges based on principles she learned not so much from her extensive academic training as from watching her father engage in civic life when she was growing up.

I'm a professor in the Department of Agricultural Economics at Purdue University. I've been here for 24 years. I was originally hired as a research associate working in the area of community development. Over time, I received my PhD and then went into a faculty-level position. We have a unit here in public policy, and we have had people working in public policy education since the 1950s. I came into this area, but then I specialized specifically in the leadership aspect of it.

I grew up on a dairy farm in central Indiana. My father was active in the community and felt strongly about giving back to the community and being a good neighbor. We used to sit around the dinner table talking and telling stories about a lot of things. My father would talk specifically about the community and what makes a community, and what makes being a good neighbor. He felt it was our responsibility to get involved in those issues that are important to building a community and its institutions. My father was on the school board during the consolidation of the schools. He also helped organize the county planning commission. Both of those issues were very polarizing and very controversial. I was a teenager at the time, and remember the hateful phone calls he got. We even had our milk poisoned and had to pour it down the drain. I saw people who we felt were our friends and neighbors say very mean and hateful things about my father around public issues. So that's what piqued my interest in this area.

My dad was a wonderful role model. He articulated a set of principles that I, at the time, didn't know were very solid public policy principles. As an adult, I've learned to respect the values that he talked about and lived in his life. I now talk about them.

One principle is to get involved. Never take our democracy for granted. He felt very strongly about that—that as a good citizen, you don't just vote, although you do that, but you get involved, and you make the community the quality of life that you want it to be. So that was first and foremost. I would see him stay at meetings until one o'clock in the morning and then turn around and get up at five to milk the cows. It was tremendous giving on his part. He didn't have an eight-to-five job.

Second, you listen to others to hear what they have to say. Third, when you speak, you make sure that you have your facts, that you've done your homework. He was very cautious about just expressing opinions that were uninformed. He felt strongly about reading everything that you could, gaining all the information that you could gain, before you spoke out and said things that were foolish. He was careful about knowing what he was talking about.

He also expressed many times that a person who may seem to be your enemy on one public issue may turn out to be your greatest ally on another. In other words, you never burn bridges. Or putting it another way, you keep the focus on the issue and never destroy a relationship. Always keep the relationship intact, particularly when it's with friends and neighbors. And with that, I think there was a lot of underlying respect for one another. With public issues, you're going to have a lot of disagreement. But you can argue and disagree with one another as long as you have that respect for one another, and keep the focus on the issue, not on the person. So those were things that were talked about in my home.

I think he learned these principles the hard way: through experience and observing other people that he admired, and ones that he didn't admire. His parents were not particularly active in public issues. He was very involved in youth groups and church as a young man, and his whole adult life was in public service. The people that he didn't admire were those who came in with just opinions, called others by names, and said things that were disrespectful. And I think that reaffirmed him in the way he acted and the ways he didn't want to act.

I did my undergraduate work at Purdue. I was the first in my family to go to college. The other members of my family are still in the rural community and still involved with the farm. I always knew I wanted to go to college because I loved school. It was just always known that I would go on to school, and so I did. I went to Purdue because I got a scholarship and it paid all my expenses. So it was a deal I couldn't refuse.

I grew up in a time where my father was a heavy influence in my life, and I can remember him saying, "You're going to meet a nice young man and get married," and that was that. I didn't have positive role models in terms of careers. My counselor in high school reinforced that, putting me in home economics because, as he told me, "You can always make a good homemaker." I came up through that. Thank goodness that has changed now!

I wanted to be an architect and go to Michigan State. They don't have a school of architecture at Purdue, so I went into interior design instead and started taking courses in sociology. I had a wonderful instructor my senior year who sat down with me and asked me what I was doing, and encouraged me to go to Cornell into urban planning. I think that is when I really started to identify what I wanted to do.

Right after I graduated from Cornell with my master's in Urban Planning, I got a position with a private consulting firm in Saratoga Springs, New York. I worked as an urban planner on two projects, writing comprehensive plans and zoning ordinances. I had a wonderful mentor who taught me how to work with people in the community. He taught me that everything is about the people and the leadership of the community. He taught me how to identify the leadership structure in a community and how to work with citizens. I spent six months there doing survey work, conducting interviews and engaging with people in terms of their values and the community. We wrote a comprehensive plan and zoning ordinances for two communities. That experience taught me how important it is to listen to people and work with them.

After these projects were completed, I came back to Indiana and got a position as a planner in an environmental engineering firm in Indianapolis. I spent two and a half years doing a little bit of everything, from working with state government agencies and writing grant proposals, to doing environmental impact assessments, and working in communities. It was a good experience, but I kept getting into trouble because I saw communities with lots of needs. I was spending a lot of time working with communities without having them under a contract. A private consulting firm is about making money, and I wasn't too concerned about making money; I was more concerned about helping people. So I got called into the president's office on several occasions to be told, "This is a consulting firm, and our business is to make money." So I found that this wasn't the niche for me.

There was a position that became available at Purdue in rural development in 1977. I applied to it and got it, and I've been here since. I worked full-time, and worked on my PhD in sociology, focusing on leadership and how it emerges in a community and how people come together to make decisions. My dissertation was on the attitudes of leaders and residents in rural Indiana communities toward change. I was looking at whether there were differences between leaders and residents. There were significant socioeconomic differences, but I found that their read on the issues in the community were not different.

Citizens Developing a Voice at the Table

I want to tell you about one of my projects, to give you a sense of what I do. The project I'm going to talk about is in a township located adjacent to the university. It's a story about how people in a community were having decisions made for them, and they had no representation on those decision-making boards. If I were to give it a title, it would be something about citizens developing a voice at the table. The initial inquiry was made in 1994, the program was conducted in 1995, and implementation started in 1996.

All the work I do is through our county Extension staff. Because I'm on the state staff, I'll frequently have people who have heard me speak call me directly. I always ask them to contact their local Extension educator, so the request comes through our local Extension office rather than to me directly. That way it engages our local educator. This request came that way. It came from a township trustee. She contacted our local Extension educator, who called me, and we talked about the situation because there were some political things going on. With it being so close to campus, I guess there's always a question of whether education will make a difference. Particularly in this situation, the educator and I discussed whether it was a good idea for us to get involved. We met with the township trustee to gain more information about what she had in mind, what the concerns were, and so forth.

There was a lot of development taking place in the township. The township is relatively well-to-do because it is located near the university. It still had areas in agricultural production, but growth was now moving into the township. The growth was taking a lot of the farmland and open space. There are also wetland areas and other natural resources. It's a very beautiful area. It has rolling hills, which in this area of the state is unusual, and people wanted to protect that. They felt that there was a lot of development going on that was not realizing those natural features.

Decisions were being made in the county and the city about the future growth and expansion of the city, and the township people were not represented. Consequently, the township trustee was upset. She contacted us for help. We had concerns initially because she clearly had a position. The other thing that concerned us is that it wasn't a group of citizens that came to us; it was one individual, a township trustee. (A township trustee in Indiana does not have a lot of authority. In Indiana, the county commissioner is the CEO of the county, so to speak. Township trustees distribute dog tags and welfare checks. If you've got a complaint, I guess you could call them, but their powers are not that great. However, they do run for public office.) So we needed to consider: to what extent is this a personal agenda? Or is this truly a public issue where education and bringing the people together to discuss the issues would make a difference?

The Extension educator and I asked her questions about what she thought was going on, about the interest level of other people, about any form of organized group of citizens that currently existed. Other than the volunteer fire department, she told us that there was no organized group, and that was one of the issues. We asked her these questions to get a better feel for what was going on, and also to gauge her level of interest in involving others in a process. And we talked with her about what we felt we could offer.

We told her that we saw our role as being facilitators and educators in a public process—that our role is that of education. We're not private consultants, and we do not make recommendations. We will bring people together and create an opportunity for citizens—and we do use that word, citizens—to come together to talk about issues and to help them look at alternative courses of action, and to facilitate a process whereby they can develop their own plan of action. But we do not make decisions for the people; we facilitate. Through that, we can provide education, and we can tap into the resources of the university to the extent that expertise may be needed. We would not be making any decisions, and we would not be making any recommendations—we would provide a process whereby they would do that. That was exactly what she wanted. So with that, we felt there was a reason for us to get involved and that we could do some meaningful work through education and organization.

We asked her to identify other people she knew who would broadly represent the township—I guess you would call it a steering committee—to help get this process under way. She identified nine to ten people and then asked them whether they would they be willing to meet with us. We met in a home, sitting around the living room talking about the issues and what they saw happening there, and what they thought needed to be done.

We met in a home because basically, there wasn't any place else to meet. In fact, that ended up being a bit of a problem as we went through this process. The only places available were an elementary school or a church. The church had pews, where it's very hard to sit in a circle because you couldn't move them, and the elementary school had teeny, weenie, little seats that were much too small for some of us. So it was a bit of a problem. But we talked about a process that we might go through to bring people together across the township. We spent a lot of time talking about the process.

We also spent a lot of time talking about how to involve the media in this process. That's usually one of the first questions people will ask. They want to leave the media out because they don't want to be misrepresented, or they don't want the media taking off on some tangent. There's a great fear of the media, I have found. But I have learned that the media are essential and wonderful if they understand what it is you're trying to do.

So coming out of that initial meeting, the steering committee and pairs of people took on particular tasks. A couple of people took the task of identifying all the subdivisions, all the neighborhoods, and every possible way that they could think of to generate a list of all the households in the township. Because there were no organized groups, that was a bit of a challenge. They literally went out to mobile home parks and to the various subdivisions to collect people's names.

Two other people took on as their task to meet with the media—the television station, the local paper, a couple of different local papers—to ask them whether they would give us coverage and to explain to them what we were going to undertake. Originally, they were not going to involve the media; I encouraged them to go talk to the media, based on my past experience. I have found that if you meet with the editor of the paper or with the reporter who covers that area, and they understand what it is that you're trying to accomplish and come in at the very beginning of the process, then they're a part of the process, and their coverage is just absolutely superb. And throughout this whole process, we had excellent media coverage.

There were another couple of people who were responsible for logistics: finding a large public place where we could meet, where people could come and we could sit around tables to talk. That was a bit of a challenge. I do feel it's important to meet in the neighborhood or in the community. As I said, we ended up meeting one time in a church that wasn't the best, but at least it was there in the township.

After the list of all the people in the townships had been attained, letters were sent out describing the process and why it was important to have their input and inviting them to participate. We had set up three 3-hour meetings that were scheduled well in advance so that people could get them on their calendars. We encouraged people to come to all three meetings, because the meetings would build upon each other. If they weren't at the first meeting, it would be a little difficult to catch up at the second. We really wanted them to take the time to be there for all three. And basically, people did. We had an excellent turnout. We had about 140 people engaged in the meetings.

If you're familiar with the "Take Charge" program, that's what we were doing. The first meeting was a chance for people in small groups to talk about what they thought were the strengths and weaknesses of their community. The small groups then reported back to the total group. Because of the size of the group, we had to have microphones that we could quickly move from table to table. It was very important for each and every table to report back, because it was important for the people to hear, "Gee I thought it was just me who was concerned about this." Or "I didn't know anybody else cared about that." It's so important for people to hear what others are thinking and feeling.

I facilitated the meeting. Part of my job is to hear what people are saying and to hear the common themes and the common threads. At the end of the meeting, I would summarize what I heard as the common threads. Each time we met, I also encouraged them to get acquainted with at least five new people, to go up and extend their hands and say, "Hello, I'm so and so. Who are you and where do you live?" I reminded them that this is a neighborhood; this is a community. The first meeting is always a little cool, because everybody doesn't know everyone. We have refreshments. Refreshments are very, very important. It's a three-hour meeting. Half-way through we break and have refreshments so that people have a chance to mingle and talk. I think that's really critical.

At the end of the first meeting, we summarized, and then we talked about what we were going to be doing at the next meeting. The second meeting was a fun meeting where we tried to get a vision for their community. We did that by breaking the room into two groups, and then we divided them into small groups. Half the room was working on their worst nightmare: if they woke up in 20 years, and this was the very worst community that they could imagine. The other half of the room was working on their best dream. Both of these are extremes, but in doing that, it helps people articulate their hopes, their dreams, their fears, their concerns. And you start to see some of the common themes that are coming out. At the end of that, I ask for three or four or five volunteers who would like to take all the information from that meeting and start to draft a vision statement. They did, and they came up with a beautiful vision statement.

The third meeting, then, we get at the issues. If this is a vision that we want to try to achieve, what are the issues that we need to address to move us toward that vision? This time, they go to tables around those issues, and they start to talk about what can be done. Some of the things that repeatedly came up were that they wanted more open space and more parks; they wanted some guarantee of those open spaces, that they wouldn't be developed. They wanted to have more say on local government bodies that were making decisions about that community. So as they were meeting at their table, they started to ask, "Okay then, how do we do this?" At the table on having a say in local government, for example, they started to talk about "Well, what could we do to have a say?" So they're starting to look at ways of working together, and they're starting to use the word *we*, so it dissipates the self-interest. And they're starting to think of community.

In another community where we used this same process—it was a community that was in conflict—we went through this, and a person stood up and said, "I've lived here all my life and I thought we were in conflict. But what's the conflict? We're all saying we want the same thing. What's our problem? Why can't we get on with it?" And it just turned the whole meeting. In this case, I didn't hear that. It was just great harmony, because there really wasn't any dissension. Everybody was saying, "Yeah, yeah, this is what we need to do."

It is at that third meeting where you start to hear people say that they have a great assurance that the issues that concern them are also issues for other people. And so now they're saying, "We really need to do something about this, and I want to help do something about it." So people who normally aren't engaged because they either don't have the opportunity or they don't know how to get engaged, now are getting engaged. Some of these people are cardiologists and upper-income people working alongside lower-income people living in the mobile home park.

At the first meeting, people will sit by people they're most comfortable with, people of their own kind. This is where I think facilitating a meeting is very important. We mixed them up from the very beginning, so they would sit with people that they didn't know and they could hear about the community from a different perspective; so that the cardiologist who drives his Mercedes could hear a lower-income person talk about the inaccessibility of the community services.

As I facilitate, I'm very open about what I'm doing. I don't facilitate in a hidden way. I tell people up front that we have mixed them because when we come into a room like this, we're all a little anxious. We don't know quite what to expect, and we're going to sit by people that we feel most comfortable with. And I tell them that I'm going to be stretching them a little bit beyond their comfort zone, and would really like for them to sit where we've assigned them: because they are friends and neighbors, and we want them to get acquainted and to listen to what others feel are issues in the community.

At that first meeting, people think, "I'd rather be sitting by my spouse or by my cousins or by people I work with." By that third meeting, I don't assign seats, and they go to tables where they don't know people. It's a fascinating dynamic because they have seen the value in it. So they start reaching out more.

Individuals have different levels of power, but I see that as people start to talk about issues in the community and what can be done, people who may not see themselves as having power find that they do have power, that they can get involved. They can gather information, they can send out the next mailing, or they can write the vision statement. So power really isn't an issue. In part, individual power isn't as strong as when people form cliques or subsets; I try to watch out for that as a facilitator so that doesn't happen. The only time I've seen it become an issue is when a group of people came—they were not in this community, but in another community— with their own agenda and were trying to get the microphone to influence the group toward their agenda. The local Extension educator knows when this is likely to happen, and ground rules can be established beforehand. The local Extension educator is critical in knowing things like that.

Because they live in the community, the Extension educator knows what groups are forming and the individuals who may have their own specific agenda. They run into these people, and they hear talk in the community before the meeting that it may happen. I really depend upon the local educator for this kind of information. It's very valuable. So before the meeting, I work with the educator to find out what's happening, or if there are any conflicts that are currently going on. For example, if it's just before an election, you know you may have political candidates trying to influence the meeting.

The other thing is the importance of having ground rules. I have ground rules at all the meetings. People normally don't know what you mean by that, so I explain that because we are here in public, each of us has views that are very, very important that need to be expressed. But we're a large number of people interacting, so it's important that we have some way of acting together in public that we can all buy into. So I will usually give them a couple of principles to get them started and then let them generate ideas for rules—things like everyone has an opportunity to speak but no one has the opportunity to dominate, that we will treat everyone with respect, that there will be no name-calling or foul language, those types of things. They come up with much stricter ground rules than I would ever come up with. We post those at each of the meetings.

In summary, a project like this begins with someone initiating a call to Extension, sometimes through me or sometimes through the local agent. In this case, it came to me, but I channeled it to the local educator to involve the local office, because that was essential. Then it's a process of whether this is an individual agenda or whether there is a legitimate public issue here that can be addressed. Can we undertake something meaningful through education, recognizing we are not private consultants? And then after that, we identify a steering committee to give leadership to the process, and our role becomes more one of coaching the process and facilitating the meetings to ensure the meetings are fair and that they're open and accessible and meaningful.

In this case, I coached the process by working very, very closely with the steering committee. I met with them frequently so that they understood the process. We met two or three times before the three meetings started. Then after each meeting, the steering committee met again. We started on a Thursday, so it was three Thursdays in a row. Then after the third meeting, we met several times to talk about what came out of the meetings, what the next steps ought to be, and how to keep communication going. Some of that was discussed at the third meeting, but they really had the responsibility for ensuring that it happened. The biggest challenge was: how do we keep everybody informed and share all information so that no one feels that someone has more information than somebody else? What mechanism do you set up to do that, particularly in an area where there were no organized groups or institutions?

What they decided to do, after that series of three meetings, was to hold a monthly meeting about issues that came out that were important. Because of the growth in the area, one of the big issues was the expansion of the school. So they had a public meeting with all three school superintendents to talk about their projections on growth and what they saw as the effects of the growth on the school system. Another month they had a meeting on local government and taxation, the effect of taxes, and how taxes finance services to that community. They set up a series of educational meetings. We provided input into those meetings and acquainted them with experts from Purdue who could talk about these issues. But they set them up and they were in charge of the meeting. We took an approach that would enable the greatest input from people and would bring to the top the issues of the people. Altogether, more than 240 people were involved in the whole thing.

The next stage is what I call studying the issues and developing a plan of action. They formed task forces around the issues that came out at that third meeting. This was a self-selection of people who had an interest in that issue and signed up for it. There were six different issues that came out, so they formed task forces around each issue. These were: (1) annexation and government; (2) fire and safety infrastructure; (3) a US highway relocation; (4) wastewater, well water, drainage, highways and bridges; (5) land-use planning and zoning; and (6) recreational development. I met with the chairpersons of those groups and did a leadership training workshop on what it means to be a chair of a group, what's expected, how you work through this process. We developed a timeline so that each of them was very clear about what was expected of them and how they were to go about doing their work. We were all in agreement on a timeline. Then those task forces did their work. They gathered information. They studied the issues. And they developed a plan of action with a set of recommendations for what they thought needed to be done.

After three or four months, we brought everyone together again. Each of those task forces gave their report to the total group, and then we put that together in a report. They shared it with decision makers—the county commissioners, the city government and so forth—and they also distributed a copy to every household in the township. Now they are proceeding to act on those recommendations. The whole process takes about one year from the time we are contacted to set up the program, we do the program, and the task forces do their work and then report back. Then there's the implementation. They're still carrying out the implementation.

Reflections

The most significant thing, I think, that came out of this project was that, in the beginning, people were viewing others as enemies. The developers were the enemies; the city government was the enemy. They've come to realize that we're all part of a community, and now they're working together. They're talking about the issues and working through the issues, rather than seeing it more as a polarized kind of thing where they say, "They're the enemy, and I'm going to fight them." I think the change comes from going through this process, having a discussion, talking about the issues, and finding that there is another way of resolving public issues without seeing it in terms of a battle. I talked very openly in the meetings about the importance of public discourse and how to do that. I do think that there is a set of skills with this that can be articulated and taught.

For example, when they were talking about how to have input on the Area Plan Commission about controversial zoning ordinances, we talked about changing the strategy from fighting the Area Plan Commission and hiring an attorney to "Let's go to the Plan Commission meetings and sit in on them and see how they operate and how they make their decisions. Let's talk with the planners and see what their plans are. Let's learn as much as we can about it." So individuals started doing that and they reported back to the others about what they learned.

I think one of our roles as Extension educators can be to suggest alternative approaches to problem-solving other than hiring an attorney and having an attorney fight it for you, which seems to be a very common mind-set. I see so many times a person has an issue and he or she tries to find allies who will fight with them. They often hire an attorney to fight their battle for them so they win, rather than seeing that "We're in a community together. We all have a stake here. Let's talk about this and work it out together around a table." That model is forgotten or not thought about. I talk about it, and then people say, "Oh, I like that." But they hadn't thought about it.

Of course, there were also challenges during this process. The township trustee who initiated this effort, was fighting some other battles. This whole effort was identified with her, and that was jeopardizing the larger program and the involvement of other people. That was of great concern to people. Another issue was the issue of leadership. The people who were on the steering committee did provide excellent leadership. The problem was they invested so much of themselves that it then became their project, and they didn't like turning over leadership to other people. I think bringing in new leadership and turning things over to others is a real challenge in any effort, and it was a challenge here. I wouldn't say that we dealt with it well, and I don't know if there is any resolution to it. We talked about it. New people sometimes don't have the investment of those who were initially involved, and so things fall through the cracks. So I would say an issue is that of leadership. The project is still with the original leadership.

A couple of things did come out that have been very significant. The group identified people to sit in on the City Council meetings, the County Commissioner meetings, the County Council meetings, the Area Plan Commission, the School Board, and other major public bodies—and asked them to be there not just when they were dealing with township issues, but every time the public body met. And if an issue was going to be discussed that affected the township, they alerted other people so that they could attend and participate. At first, that was very, very threatening to the elected officials. They didn't know what these people were about and thought they were there to cause trouble. But they found that they were there to learn and to listen and to support and sometimes to ask questions, particularly when it affected the township. So that's become a standard practice now. The township leaders also developed a newsletter, which goes out once a month to all the residents in the township that keeps them apprised of all the public issues that are going on and gives them the dates and times and meeting places of all the meetings. That's been very positive. Now an e-mail group has formed among those who have e-mail, and they have constant communication going on around issues.

One of the big challenges in this work is the implementation of action plans. With all good intentions, it's so hard to carry forward on a volunteer basis. This community has continued to work together over a six-year period, but people are burning out. They're in a bit of a Catch-22. They are getting weary, yet don't want to hand over the leadership to others. But they have taken it upon themselves to continue to communicate, and get involved, and keep everybody informed and so forth for six years, which is pretty phenomenal. I've got two big accordion file folders of their news-letters up here.

The work I've been describing to you is educational work, as I see it. I define education very broadly. It's a two-way street of someone from the university in a facilitating role learning about the community along with the citizens, as they are learning from one another. It's people educating one another about the community. One of my aims in the process is to hear the conversation go from "I, mine, and me" to "we," when people recognize "Yes, it is an issue that affects me, but it's also an issue that affects us." It's the notion that we all live in community. It was very important to me to listen for that.

Another aim is tolerance and respect for one another as neighbors. In this community, that was not an issue. In some other communities I've worked in, it has been a real issue. So I listen to the conversations, and when I see people starting to work together respectfully, it is an important achievement. Also, I'm hoping that people learn a process and a way of working together—that regardless of the issue, they've learned how to talk about public issues with civility and how to work them through any problem-solving model. So it's not just about the issue that they were talking about five years ago, but they can apply that process to an issue today and five years down the road. I also hope they recognize that there are other approaches besides building allies, forming a special-interest group, and fighting. There's a better way through collaboration. Those are some of the things that, for me, were most important in this work.

Personally most important are my own skills and abilities to model all of it. That's a real challenge. It's one thing to teach it; it's something entirely different to model it. Do I always listen? Am I always tolerant? To what extent are my biases creeping into what I say and how I say it? That's the personal challenge.

I think this work is absolutely fundamental to the land-grant mission and to Extension. Just yesterday, we formed a public issues group here to look at our future at the university. I think our mission is about helping people solve their own problems and taking responsibility for their own issues. To me, that's the highest form of education. It's not just transferring expertise. Education, to me, comes with a discourse. It comes with a much deeper understanding of issues. You get in community, where you're talking with people who have very different views. You keep talking and keep talking until everyone around the table has seen the light bulb go on, because "Now I'm looking at this issue differently than just in my own little narrow slice of the world." That, to me, is the highest level of education. It's the deepest level of education. It's not just basic research coming out of the laboratory. That's important, and we must continue doing that as a university. But what concerns me is when the pendulum swings totally in that direction, cutting out this whole other piece of our civic responsibility to the public and to our democracy. Having spent a lot of time in the former Communist countries, I know how very, very fragile our democracy is. I think the university plays a very critical role in helping safeguard that by creating opportunities for people to come together and have those light bulb experiences as they're sitting around the table with people who come at the issue from a very different point of view.

The thing that scares me so much about the university—I said this yesterday publicly and I went home in agony last night because I think I say too much sometimes—is when I hear people from the university say, "But we have to educate those people about 'The Truth,'" meaning that "The Truth" is what they have come up with in their piece of research. That's scary. It's very scary. My definition of education is much broader, and I think it's much deeper and richer, and it stretches us. I think it stretches us to learn tolerance in listening to people who have very different values, or who are of different political persuasions, and to listen to that and think about it. To me, that's when you're getting the butterflies in the tummy and the sweaty armpits, because it's making you uncomfortable. That, to me, is what education is about. But it's not the typical view in the university, as I heard yesterday.

I've had a real struggle doing this kind of work. I've often felt marginalized and on the fringe. (Still, I did get promoted and tenured.) I've always felt that individuals who work at the margins have the greatest freedom to do what they want to do. I would say that I've marched to my own drum here, and the institution allowed me to do it because I had so much citizen support. The administrators hear from the public.

Are they going to put resources into this kind of work? No way. It's very much a research institution, and people are getting the benefits of bringing in research dollars, and that's pretty much basic science and research. So unfortunately, I don't see resources being allocated to this area of work. But I just think this work is terribly important because it's offering so much to communities that are hungry for new approaches. I think there is a real hunger out there, but I don't think people know how to go about it. They don't have the opportunity. I see my role as providing opportunities and a way to deal with public issues in a different way.

My appointment is 100 percent Extension. Right now, in this department, we are toying with bringing public issues education into the classroom. A number of us here in the department have had informal conversations. And new staff who have come on board are starting to challenge some of the older ways of teaching and thinking. They see the need. I'm very, very excited about this, about integrating what we do more into the students' lives and work. It's not enough to just come out of the university with technical competence. Students also should know how to work with others around controversial issues, develop tolerance of different points of view, develop critical thinking skills, and work through differences. We're not there yet. But I'm very excited that there's at least an openness to this possibility and we're talking about it.

I regret not spending more time writing about my work. I think one area of research that would be fascinating, for example, is to measure the social and economic costs of resolving public issues through special interest groups' legal battles. I don't know quite how to undertake this, but my hunch is that it's far more expensive, and the results aren't as satisfying. I've undertaken this collaborative process in about 40 communities, and they keep me informed about what happens. The reason I use this process is because I find it works.

Interview conducted by Scott J. Peters

Not an Expert but a Catalyst

A Profile of Joe Sumners
Director, Economic & Community Development Institute
Auburn University

In this profile Joe Sumners offers a candid account of a key episode in the evolution of his work as an academic professional with community and economic development responsibilities. He tells a story of how a particularly painful failure led him and his colleagues in Alabama to shift their main roles, stepping back from their roles as experts to become, instead, catalysts. Based on this and other experiences, he draws an important lesson: Extension's real "competitive  *advantage" isn't the provision of "research-based knowledge" as many people often assume and proclaim. Rather, it's the public relationships that people have built over time in nearly every county in the nation. This and other lessons from Joe's work help us see Extension's potential for bringing people together across lines of difference for productive and deliberative public work.*

My name is Joe Sumners and I am the director of the Economic & Community Development Institute (ECDI) at Auburn University. I came to this position in 2000 as director of the Economic Development Institute (EDI), which, at that time, was under our vice president for University Outreach. In 2006, we had a reorganization on campus and

EDI assumed responsibility for directing the community development program for the Alabama Cooperative Extension System. We were renamed ECDI and combined the staff and resources of both EDI and Extension's Community Resource Development Program. Now ECDI provides leadership for community and economic development for both our university and Alabama Extension.

With regard to my responsibilities, I provide direction for the unit. We provide educational programs, leadership training, community planning, and other kinds of engagement initiatives. Also, we conduct applied and policy research, and produce publications on various topics related to economic and community development. We have done a good bit of work in the area of rural development and have issued several reports related to that. Another program area for us is community assistance. We do quite a bit of strategic planning work with communities. We do other kinds of engagement projects and activities, such as deliberative forums, round tables, and town meetings. Altogether, we are involved in many programs and activities to assist Alabama communities.

Despite its many shortcomings, I love Alabama. It is my home. I grew up in a little community called Creswell, which is in Shelby County, Alabama. Shelby County is now the state's most prosperous county, but the wealth is mostly concentrated in the northern part of the county. I grew up in the southern part, where it was, and still is, very rural. I looked out of my front window and saw cotton fields, looked out the back window and saw a cow pasture and pond. Within a few hundred yards of our house, there was a little country church with an outhouse where my cousin and I used to go sometimes and smoke cigars. It was an interesting place to grow up.

When I started school in that area, the schools were segregated. The schools finally integrated around 1968. I was in the sixth grade, and the community experienced raw, racial tensions. There were fights in the high school between the black and white kids. It was a very difficult time.

Throughout my life, the issue of race has had a huge influence on life and politics in Alabama. I would say that my parents were sort of outliers because they were politically moderate for the times. They believed that everyone was equal in the sight of God and that everyone should have the same opportunities. My parents had a great influence on me as a kid growing up in a region where racial tolerance was the exception.

I had to decide, as a young man, how to navigate these tensions in our community. I played football and basketball on integrated teams and developed friendships with black students. So did other white kids. We began to watch people who had never interacted with the other race learn to know one another, and become friends. While some did remain hard-core racists, for many others in my school, it was hard to hold on to the hate when you actually got to know the person. That was a lesson that has stayed with me.

I left Shelby County in 1975 for Auburn University. I made very good grades as a student at Auburn, but I had trouble finding a job after I graduated. I thought that people would be knocking down doors looking for somebody just like me, but that did not turn out to be the case. It was 1979, and the economy was not in great shape. I ended up teaching high school for a while at a small private school. I taught government and civics, and coached junior high football and basketball. I really loved that job, but it didn't pay very much, so I found another job working for the county health department. I would go out and inspect dairies or septic tank installations. I stayed in that job for a couple years as an environmentalist.

I went back to Auburn to get a graduate degree, because I knew that I really wanted to do something more. Whether it was to teach or something else, I knew that I needed a graduate degree to get there. Therefore, I went to Auburn to pursue a master's degree in political science.

I began my professional career working at Auburn with the Center for Governmental Services (CGS) in 1984 after getting my master's degree. I worked there three years before leaving for the University of Georgia to pursue my doctorate. I returned to Auburn in the summers to work for CGS. After leaving Georgia, I taught political science and public administration for two years at the University of Alabama at Birmingham and one year at Stephen F. Austin State University in Nacogdoches, Texas. I got the chance to return to Auburn and CGS in 1994, and served as research and training coordinator there for seven years. While I loved teaching and research, I was thrilled to get the chance to return to work in university outreach.

While I was at CGS, we had a strong director, Keith Ward, who had a real passion for outreach and public service. He had a huge influence on who—and where—I am today. It was through working with Keith that I really developed my own passion for university outreach, and for using the resources of the university to bring about positive change in the state. Keith believed that we had an obligation and an opportunity to make a difference, and he was all about doing that. My early interest in things like tax reform and constitutional reform came from his interest in those things. From him I learned that we can make a difference. I do not know whether I would be in outreach doing the kind of things I am doing without his example. He was a director, and now I am a director. I have the same kind of orientation—that we have an obligation as a land-grant university to go out and make a difference and improve the quality of life for the people in the state in any way we can. I love my job in university outreach. I like the idea of going out and actually working with people in communities and maybe making a positive difference in people's lives.

What motivated me then, and still does, is the desire to change Alabama for the better. I feel that everything I do should have some connection to building a state that is more prosperous and progressive—a place with effective government and opportunities for folks to have good jobs and improve the lives of their families. I spent a lot of my time early in my career working on major reform initiatives for the state, such as comprehensive tax reform and constitutional reform. I thought if we could conquer those big issues, then we could change our state for the better. However, while we did great research and outreach work around these issues, not much really changed.

Consequently, I changed my focus—but not my passion. I still wanted to change Alabama, but now I believed that the real change was less likely to come from the state legislature. I had "beat my head against a wall" long enough to know that I might invest my entire career in futile attempts to get these folks to change their mind on big issues. I adopted the view that instead of thinking big, we need to think small. We can change the state for the better by focusing at the local level, community by community. I really believe that if we can focus on individual communities, then we have a chance to really make a difference through things like community planning and leadership, citizen engagement, and stakeholder connections. If we can begin to do that, then we will see stronger communities, and thus, a stronger state—a better state.

A lot of this shift in my thinking can be attributed to my work with the Kettering Foundation, which started back in 1995. I partnered with Kettering and its president, David Mathews, who is an Alabama native. We worked together in organizing a statewide town hall meeting on constitutional reform, and in developing an issue guide about Alabama state and local government that was to be used in high schools.

While working on these projects, I made many trips to Dayton, Ohio, for Kettering Foundation meetings. However, early on I was not a "true believer" in their deliberative approach, because my orientation had always been about action, not talk. I wanted to see results. So to me, there was always a feeling that there was a lot of talk, but not enough action. It was not until I really began to work in community and economic development that I came to see the value of Kettering's approach. You really cannot take action and achieve results until the right people are engaged and moving in a common direction. The folks who are making decisions and doing the work need to be talking with one another, looking at all of their options together, and finding common ground for action. Over time, I really became a true believer that positive change in communities requires people to begin getting together in a public space and interacting and talking and learning from one another.

Many of these lessons came from our community work in Alabama's "Black Belt" region. In Alabama, generally, the Black Belt is an area that begins in the western part of the state and swings down to the central part

81

of the state. It is the region where cotton was once king. The Black Belt is the footprint of slavery on the state and, really, throughout the South. It was where we had the plantation economy. Not coincidently, it is the area where there is a large black population. It also has high levels of persistent poverty, low educational attainment, and other serious challenges, which makes it just the kind of place that I like to work.

Most of the communities there are as racially segregated now as they were in 1965. In much of the Black Belt the public schools are almost 100 percent black, while whites go to private academies. The consequences for that are similar to what I saw growing up in Shelby County: the communities are divided and people do not work together. Not only do you divide the schools by race, but you also divide the community. Blacks and whites rarely interact with one another, and communities lack the civic infrastructure or cohesion they need to be successful.

There are, however, a couple of anomalies in the Black Belt, where the community tends to have a thriving local economy. Examples can be found in Demopolis and Thomasville. Those are the two bright stars in the Alabama Black Belt. It is no coincidence that, at the time of school desegregation, these two communities decided to maintain quality, integrated public schools. Today, they are relatively prosperous and seen as examples of the way things should work. From the start, leaders in these two communities said, "We are not going to divide; we are going to work together." The lesson to be learned from this is that communities cannot afford destructive division. These rural communities already have limited assets: small populations, small labor pools, and limited tax resources. Thus, they can't afford to waste anything. By dividing up into little cliques or cleavages within the community, these groups are making it harder to survive. The communities that work together despite race or class are the ones that make it. The ones that divide are going to fail.

The Uniontown Project

One experience that put this idea into practice was our work in Uniontown, Alabama, a small community located in the Black Belt. Back in 1999, when I was still with the Center for Governmental Services, I was asked to collaborate on an initiative working in Uniontown to help them coordinate a strategic planning project. The mayor of Uniontown had contacted David Wilson, who was then the Vice President for Outreach at Auburn and an African American who grew up in a neighboring county. He had made support for the Black Belt region a high priority for University Outreach. The mayor told Wilson, "We are a community that needs help," and Wilson committed Auburn to do what we could.

I went into the community to conduct a strategic planning process. The mayor appointed the members of the strategic planning committee, and we helped them develop strategies. Once we got into that process and created the plan, we realized that there were things that couldn't be done by the local government.

In that community, at the time, there were no civic groups and there were not many opportunities for folks to be engaged in doing things to help the community. Because of this, we decided that it would be a good idea to create a community development corporation (CDC), so residents could begin to seek grants and do things to invest in their community. The mayor served as the president of the CDC, and he appointed all of its members. Throughout that process, what we noticed was that people who attended those meetings would defer to the mayor, and they would expect him to have the answers to whatever problems they had. Or they would look to us as the outside experts to make decisions. They were reluctant to speak their own minds and voice their own opinions.

Well, not many months after that process began, there was an election in the community, and the mayor was defeated. In terms of our efforts, we were back at square one. All of the things we had done had been worked through the mayor: the strategic plan and the CDC. The new mayor had no use for those things.

So not exactly knowing what to do, we decided we would get some folks from the community together to talk about where we were and where we might go. We decided to recruit a representative focus group of local residents who would just come together and talk. We wanted the group to include both blacks and whites.

We thought, "How can we engage people who would come to a meeting to figure out what we do in the community?" We first identified local people who we already knew, but we realized that was too small a circle. So we went to the pastors and asked, "Could you get some folks from your church who would come to this meeting?" We went out on the streets in Uniontown and asked local residents we encountered, "Would you be interested in attending a meeting to talk about the future of Uniontown?" It really was not a scientific sampling of the community, but we got as many people as we could. We made an effort to make sure that we got both whites and blacks there by going to both the white churches and the black churches in the community and asking them to participate. That strategy was how we originally got people to the table. The area was racially divided, and many of those folks in that very small town—black and white— did not know one another and did not interact with one another. This was the first time they actually sat down together in a meeting.

We began in a small room in the city hall. During the first meeting, the chairs were arranged in rows, and the whites would sit in the front, while the blacks sat in the back. It was an interesting dynamic. We noticed that the whites would speak out, and most blacks would tend to defer to the whites who were present. As the meetings progressed though, there was a lot more interaction and a lot more learning and listening, and we began to see that people of different races were sitting together. We moved the chairs into a circle so they could see one another. The dynamics changed as the folks began to know, listen to, and trust each other.

We began with a very simple idea. We asked two questions: "What do you like about this place?" and "What would you like to change?" As the group talked, the first thing we noticed was that it did not matter whether someone was black or white; they tended to like the same things. We noted the same thing when we asked what they would like to change. As they began to talk, the group found that, while they had focused much of their lives on things that divided them, they actually had a lot in common.

84

Many great relationships were built among people who had not known one another before. They wanted to keep the meetings going, so they created a name for their group. They called themselves "Uniontown Cares." They later created an actual nonprofit organization so that they could accept money and fund projects. They set up a regular schedule for where and when they would meet. They had developed a "public space" for deliberation. Early on, they met every week on Tuesday nights at the city hall. Later, when the group got too large, they moved their meetings to the public library.

One of the things that came up in the meetings was that the area was not very attractive, and there was litter on the street. In addition, they discussed a problem they had with loitering. There were folks, especially young people, who were out on the streets, which made many people fearful. Uniontown seemed like a dangerous place, and people were scared of being in town. They knew that they could never attract economic development unless the place looked safe and attractive.

The group began to talk about this issue and they decided to go to the police chief and the mayor and get them to enact loitering laws. Once they found that there were already loitering laws in the books, they decided to make signs that said "No Loitering." Later on, through further deliberation, they discovered that many of these folks who were loitering were people they knew—their nephews, friends of their children. They were often loitering because they had alcohol or substance abuse problems. Uniontown Cares members began to ask themselves, "Well, what could be done about that?" They decided they could create an Alcoholics Anonymous group, and they did that.

The observation there, for those of us at Auburn who were working with the community, was that they had transitioned from looking for someone else to solve their problems to figuring out that they could solve problems on their own. They actually *renamed* the issue from "loitering" to "alcohol abuse," and they reframed it in such a way that they could actually do something about it. They began to say, "We are not going to worry about what the experts from Auburn can do for us. We are not going to worry about what the mayor is going to do for us. <u>We are going to see what *we* can do working together</u>." They began to develop the attitude, "We do not care what anybody else does. We are going to work together."

As they began to do little things to make a difference, they began to identify other opportunities in the community, like cleaning playgrounds, raising money for the volunteer fire department, cleaning up an overgrown African American cemetery, and organizing parades. They weren't just talking. They were *doing* things. They experienced many successes, which gave the folks engaged in the process a sense of accomplishment and pride. They started to believe that they really had the power to change things in the community.

As an outsider looking in at Uniontown, I could see that before these initiatives there was a sense of hopelessness. They had absolutely no expectations for their community and certainly no idea that they could do anything to make things better. Through their experience with Uniontown Cares, local residents became excited. As they began to undertake small projects, they developed a real sense of accomplishment. They were able to say, "We did this. Working together, we can get things done. We are the answer to the problems that we see in this community." <u>They began to feel a real sense of empowerment, and it was really a neat thing to see.</u>

Over time, they got the elected officials to pay attention and work with them. They began to see that they had more power than they had ever imagined—<u>not just individually, but collectively</u>. They realized that if they came together as a group, people would listen, pay attention to them, and even do things they wanted done. Uniontown Cares really grew until they got a lot of people involved in what they were doing. The most rewarding thing for us was <u>to see the sense of empowerment that came from the engagement process.</u>

The Uniontown project was not a complete success. There were problems. As the group grew and experienced some success, they decided that they needed some structure and organization. We helped them create a 501(c)(3) nonprofit organization, "Uniontown Cares," so they could go out and solicit funds. Of course, they had to have a board of directors. They had to have a president and officers. So they began to develop a structure. As they began to focus more on structure and organization, they began to have disagreements about who was going to be the president and how elections would be handled. They began to focus on what should be in the bylaws.

Additionally, within the group there was a difference of opinion among some folks about who should be a member of the group. They had developed t-shirts, a logo, and an identity, and it was like, "Wait a minute, do they deserve to come in and be with us?" It began to be almost like a little club. They developed status in the community from being a member, and they didn't know if they wanted to share that status with other people.

As they began to focus on issues like who was in charge and who was a member, they did less and less within the community. They didn't have as many projects. I think the biggest failing—and I think that we were culpable in this—was they were not deliberating and reflecting. They were not actually sitting and talking about things. They had a checklist of activities: "I'll do this; you do that." They really weren't thinking, "What kind of community do we want to have? And what's our role in that?" They weren't reflecting on what they had accomplished or how they had done it by talking and working together. Instead, they became very task-oriented and structure-oriented. They began to lose sight of what it was that made them so special, which was that they were actually all working together and doing good things in the community. They began to lose some of their momentum.

Reflections

I think the Uniontown project had a positive impact on the community. But even more, I believe it changed us. We learned a lot about how strong communities are built, and especially the importance of citizen deliberation and engagement. Another lesson for us was that we have a role to play in facilitating this kind of engagement and empowerment. It began to redefine for us what we could do in a community. We had seen our role as going in to provide help: technical assistance and strategic planning. We thought we could help the community grow and develop by applying our expertise. As we got into this process, we found that success was not based on our research-based university expertise. The most impactful thing we could do was to simply provide a space and facilitation for local folks to begin to think about what they might do *on their own*. We could *help folks engage*, and the results of that could be pretty powerful. From that, we really have reoriented our work to try to do more and more in terms of facilitating engagement and connections, because we believe this provides the civic infrastructure essential to building a strong community.

The Uniontown project set us on a path to do the kind of things that we are doing now, and today we are making a real difference. We are seeing change. We are seeing that communities are recognizing the vital role of engagement. We are seeing economic developers beginning to understand the importance of community development and engagement.

As a result of the Uniontown experience, we have tried to figure out how we work in communities and what we should be doing to advance economic development. Where can we make a difference? What is the area where nobody is really paying enough attention? We moved into the areas where we felt there was the greatest need and the biggest gap in service. Community development, civic engagement, and rural development is where we staked our claim. We were going to make a difference for rural Alabama and our challenged communities. We were going to focus on the community, and we were going to focus on engagement. That has informed all of the things that we do.

As I reflect, one of the lessons that I learned deals with how universities engage communities. I think the most typical kind of university-community relationship is one-way, where university knowledge, education, and expertise are used to try to solve problems in communities. I think the "expert" role described our attitude as we first went into Uniontown. I think what we have learned is that there is another role that we have to play in communities. That role is not expert, but catalyst—a facilitator who understands that the people in the communities have assets of their own, and if we can help them just see and unleash their own capacities, they can solve the problems themselves. If that is the case, it will be much more sustainable than simply an expert coming in to try to deal with a particular problem. If you can get the people in the community engaged in solving their own problems, then that's like the old adage of teaching a person how to fish rather than giving a person a fish. Before our work with Kettering and Uniontown, we were too often engaged in giving people fish rather than teaching them how to fish.

The truth is, issues like economic development, poverty, race relations, and workforce development—and other issues for which there is no simple solution that a single expert can provide—are not really subject to the kind of tools in our normal "bag of tricks." We have to go in with a little more humility, understand our limits, and often simply provide space and serve as catalysts. We have to help people in communities figure out that, if they talk together and work together, they can do a lot of things to solve their own problems. We have to listen.

Once community members begin to work together to solve their own problems, then others are more likely to want to help. External resources will have something to connect to, and they can be leveraged for greater impact. In the Black Belt and other places with deep-rooted systemic challenges, we've seen over time that billions of dollars have been invested without evidence of significant results. My feeling is that this happens because there's not a lot of internal capacity—the community and the relationships that define it aren't strong enough to leverage these external resources. On the other hand, if a community is truly engaged and has a strong civic infrastructure, external resources will have something to connect to and build upon, and can be much more effective.

I've been doing this work for about 25 years. In my roles in both outreach and Extension, one of the things that I have found, whether working with governments or in communities, is that there are great things going on in schools, government, business, the chambers of commerce, and other segments of the community. However, communities rarely get all of their assets moving in the same direction and working together. There is a general problem of disconnectedness. Unfortunately, it is rare to find community actors working in concert with one another.

The implications for Extension and university outreach are huge. I think the lessons that we learned in Uniontown present a fantastic opportunity, especially for Extension, because of the advantages of the vast Extension network. In Alabama, there is a County Extension Coordinator in each of our 67 counties. This is true for many other states as well. If Extension could do the kind of things that we're talking about, which is to serve as a facilitator, someone who listens, engages, and connects, that would be an invaluable role. It would make Extension much more relevant within our counties and communities. This is something I think Extension should be doing. This is something it can do well.

There really is no other entity in this state that has that kind of a presence in every county. In Extension, you have people who are actually embedded in the county—but also not a part of any kind of existing organizational structure, whether it's the schools, the churches, or the government. They're both inside the community and trusted outsiders as well. So they are in a perfect position to play that connecting/facilitating role in communities, something that is so badly needed.

I believe that Cooperative Extension should have a bigger role in building communities and engaging folks. There's sometimes talk among people in Extension here in Alabama about "our competitive advantage." Often it's said the competitive advantage that we have in Extension is that we have research-based knowledge that we provide folks. I agree that that is important. But after spending almost a decade in Extension, I believe the real competitive advantage is its *relationships*. Extension's value is in the relationships that it has built over time in counties and communities.

If Extension will understand its value in building communities—connecting stakeholders and engaging citizens—I think that it can be a much more relevant and powerful mechanism for changing Alabama. My vision for both Extension and university outreach is that we might play the role of connector for those various sectors and stakeholders to get them talking to one another and figuring out how to help one another, and how they can move together in the same direction. I think that's a big need, and I think it's a need that universities, and especially Extension, can and should meet.

Strategic planning is another important way that we're involved with communities. I've been doing strategic planning consulting for almost my entire career, and I love the process. You go into a community and engage people from all walks of life, such as the school superintendent, the mayor, a pastor, business leaders, and everyday citizens. You get all of these people together around a table, and you ask fundamental questions. Where are we as a community? Where do we want to go? How do we get from where we are to where we want to go? What a wonderful and important process to go through for a community! I've always loved it.

In strategic planning, the failure we often see in communities is that once the strategic planning process is over, people think they're through. They may have a document or a plan but have failed to recognize the value of the process itself. If we could create in communities an ongoing planning process where people continue to come together from various walks of life to ask how they can work together to improve their community, then I think we would have something invaluable. Communities should develop a structure in which people from various stakeholder groups come together on a regular basis and meet, plan, develop measures of progress, and figure out how to work together to build and maintain a stronger community. This is another area where I think Extension and university outreach can help.

I am a father and a grandfather. I hope that if my children and grandchildren choose to stay in Alabama, they will have a different kind of environment to grow up in than I did. If you look at all of the measures of economic prosperity, we're at or near the bottom. I think that Alabama has the potential to be so much better. That motivates me. We can and must do better. However, we have been our own worst enemy in this state. As Pogo, Walt Kelly's comic strip character, said, "We have met the enemy, and he is us." We have to figure out how we can work together in this state and in our local communities. We have many resources and assets that we don't use to their maximum potential, because we don't connect them.

Overall, I'm optimistic. I see so many opportunities for positive change in Alabama. I believe that the university has an important role to play in fostering that change. I love what I do and can't imagine a better job.

Interview conducted by Theodore R. Alter

Postscript—In October 2015, Joe Sumners was named executive director of the Government & Economic Development Institute (GEDI), a new Auburn University outreach unit. While the former ECDI was a part of the Alabama Cooperative Extension System structure, GEDI is not.

Devotion to the Cause

A Profile of Katrina Easley
County Extension Coordinator, Perry County Extension Office
Alabama Cooperative Extension, Auburn University

In this profile Katrina Easley tells a story of a profound turning point in her life that came during her work with a youth leadership development project in Perry County, Alabama. The youth helped restore her sense of hope for the future of the county she was born and raised in, and still lives in and loves. She pairs this story with a less positive experience she had at the same time with an adult leadership development project. She offers insights and lessons related to the successes and difficulties she encountered with both youth and adults, including the problem of people coming "to the table of deliberation wearing masks of feigned cooperation, only to remove them at night when the meetings are over." Her core lesson, as she puts it, is that "we have to know that if we want to change anything for the better, it's going to take devotion to the cause." Her voice, throughout this profile, reveals her unshakable devotion to the cause of bringing citizens together—young and not so young—to make their neighborhoods and communities better.

My name is Katrina Easley, and I am the county Extension coordinator for the Perry County Extension Office, which is a branch of Alabama A&M and Auburn University's Alabama Cooperative Extension System. I have been employed with the Extension System for eight years, three of

93

which I've served as coordinator. I've been told that I was the first individual in Cooperative Extension to move from a support staff position to management status. I was the secretary in the office that I manage. It was a great transition—a big transition—and it's been both challenging and rewarding to perform two different roles for the same organization. Altogether, I enjoy what I'm doing, as I did before, but now I find dealing with the public can often bring more challenges than I anticipated prior to taking this position.

Before I joined the Extension system, I was on the road roughly two and a half hours a day, commuting from Perry County to Tuscaloosa County. But the commute began to take its toll. I'm the mother of three children, so that in itself posed a challenge for me. The children wanted to participate in community events and play Little League sports, but it was difficult to get someone to take my kids to practice and games each afternoon while my husband and I were working away from home. Eventually, I began to feel guilty and decided I needed to be home to help my children appreciate their childhood.

For this reason, I started looking for a job in Perry County for the first time. I heard about the position at the Extension office and applied. After I got the job, I began to realize how much I enjoyed it. In life, there are people who become important influences on your work and thinking. For me, that person was my supervisor. He was a mentor for me, and he encouraged me to go back to school. I had always wanted to get my bachelor's degree, but until that moment, I hadn't felt the confidence to do so. Of course, family would encourage and support me no matter what, but to have someone outside of that environment recognize my potential made a huge difference. He would always say, "You should always want to be in a position to move up, and if not, have an option to leave with opportunity." Unfortunately, he later became ill and passed away. So the position of county Extension coordinator opened up.

Initially, no one applied. However, after Auburn agreed to change the title to "in-training," I was able to submit my application. Having been the secretary for five years, I thought, "Why not? Let's try it and see what happens." So I did and was rewarded with the opportunity to serve as the county Extension coordinator. As the secretary, I thought I knew the role because I assumed we were the frontline. Oftentimes secretaries are. But after getting the job, I realized how much goes on behind the scenes.

No two days are the same. In any given week, I may be fulfilling a different function every day. Sometimes I wear a different hat each day of the week. Tasks that I oversee range from human health and diet and nutrition, to youth and community development. Each of these roles involves working with a variety of county residents. With regard to health education, I participate in a weekly radio broadcast that informs community members about pressing health issues, updates, and things of that nature. My work with youth development has led me to engage with fifth-grade students across the county, usually twice a month. I meet them in their classrooms to do educational programs that correspond to whatever the teacher is already instructing them in. Here in Perry County, we are in the top third percentile concerning childhood obesity within the state of Alabama, and we're using that as an opportunity to work with children to get them to become more physically engaged. Every week, on Thursday and Friday, we provide a fun activity as well as a healthy snack for the kids, getting them physically active and then talking about the importance of the drink choice. Oftentimes, I just reiterate the importance of physical activity, and I use that as an avenue to teach our children the value of healthier lifestyles and the importance of exercise. All of this depends on what my schedule is like, and what programs our county is considering within that particular time frame.

Chiefly, what motivates the work that I do is the fact that I am a product of Perry County. I was born and raised here, and I am the product of the county school system. I know that it works. I am also the mother of three children, and they're a part of the community as well. I would love nothing more than for them to make Perry County their home. Yet when I look at the opportunities that they would have in their adult lives, there are very few. Therefore, I'm inspired to keep our younger generation here in the community and to do whatever it takes to generate revenue and opportunities—to create an economic base for their future. I will work with whatever agency or group that can help stimulate the growth of our county's financial system so that our children will remain here in later years. I want to see some growth in our community. I want our towns to be clean and vibrant. I want to see flowers and sidewalks. These are all simple things, but they would make a big impact. If our children have an opportunity to experience a better Perry County, then all of this work will have been worth it.

I look at my youthful years in comparison to my children's, and I see a major difference. Not just in the television shows and music, but in the aesthetics of our community. We had activities for children to engage in growing up. There were two parks that we could go and visit. Kids played ball against other individuals during that time. But now as I look at my children, we don't have those opportunities anymore. The neighborhood park has been bought by a private agency, and a fence now surrounds it because it's deemed private property. In my youth, I used to complain that I didn't have a lot to do. But in comparison to the recreation offered to my kids, I had plenty to do.

Contrary to the situation today, years ago we would have community parties where we didn't have to worry about violence and safety, which is a major issue today. The parents would get together and have events for their children—community events. Now everything is "you take care of your own, and I'll take care of mine." There's a great difference that I see between growing up when I was young and the youth today. Overall, the problem lies in our failure as parents to take the initiative and begin to work on the problems at hand.

Youth and Adult Leadership Development in Perry County

One particular experience that had a profound impact on my thinking was an opportunity I was given to do a youth leadership program in Perry County. I worked with 23 students from local schools, and we shared in-depth training sessions, leadership seminars, and other developmental activities. Of course, there were many challenges that came along with this program. For instance, I found it difficult to work out an ideal setting for the event to take place. Because the kids were already involved in school activities, we couldn't simply pull them out to participate. Nevertheless, I wouldn't let that stop me. I needed to work with these children, and I had to find a way to do it. After I'd weighed all of my options, I decided to talk to some teachers and the principals, and I asked them to collaborate in bringing the program to life. Together, we decided that the best way to go about it was to meet on Saturdays. That way we didn't have to coordinate with the schools and we could deal directly with the parents. So that's what I did.

During the time the program took place, the children bonded, and they grasped the concept of unity and cooperation. When it was time for them to graduate from the youth leadership program, we asked them who they would like to invite to come and serve as a keynote speaker. To my surprise, the students told me they didn't want to invite a speaker. I asked them why not, and they said that they wanted to speak themselves! They wanted to invite their principals, teachers, and other members of the community because they realized I had to seek funding for my position through our local government agency, which is our county commission. They did their own keynote address, and it was from that point on that I realized the impact that this one, small youth leadership group had on those students.

From there, I received calls from parents asking how they could get their children involved in the program. We received a lot of press on the event, and it was printed in the local newspapers. Some of the children posted it online, and we got calls from other students asking to be a part of the group. In the end, despite the fact that I wasn't from the same town as some of these student's families, the parents decided to enroll their children in our program for the sake of community development.

Stories like that motivate me to continue doing my work. If I can't reach the adults, I don't worry about it. Maybe I should, but I don't, because as adults, we are sometimes too complacent. Too many of us want it to be this way or no way. In contrast, when I reach out to the youth and work with them, they always walk out with a different vision than adults. That's inspiration for me to emphasize the importance of children.

I got a phone call recently from one of our funding sources, and they asked me what was going on. I said that I didn't have any money and that it takes money to operate the program. They asked me if I requested the money, and I said that I'd asked for it earlier on but I hadn't heard anything. Then they told me to simply request it again. That was extremely rewarding: to hear a commissioner call me and say that the funding would be made available. They saw the benefit of the program and wanted the children to be as involved as possible; motivation for me to continue the work I've started.

Nevertheless, whereas the youth leadership program provided a positive example of what Cooperative Extension can produce, there have been a few negative experiences, as well. A particular project that comes to mind is one that dealt with adult leadership in Perry County. My role in the project was coordinator, but I also served as a student in the adult leadership class. So it was a twofold experience. We encountered a wide variety of participants who ranged from one end of the professional spectrum to the other. For example, local business owners sent a few employees to participate, but we also had bankers and an elected official involved in the program. Everyone who was a member of the class came from a different background. Their presence was meant to educate them, and the purpose of the course was to inform them on community affairs with respect to education, economic and community development, and health care. In sum, we wanted to look at our county and decide how it could be made better.

Overall, we attempted to engage citizens as much as possible. That's why we visited local schools, to deduce what needed our attention most. It was about finding ways to impact policies and programs going on both individually and collectively. We wanted to connect with those who had signed up for the leadership programs, and we focused on doing this with regard to government affairs—primarily because we're in an era in which everything comes down to elected officials. The course sought to inform and educate the students enough so that when an election came around, they would be aware of the qualifications necessary for the position in question.

Getting citizens together and making them feel empowered is a powerful tool. It shows them that they can have a direct impact on the world around them. We began by holding dialogues about big issues in Perry County. For example, there is no dialysis center in our community; yet, we have at least 50 to 70 individuals traveling out of the county on a daily basis to receive dialysis treatment in either Marengo or Dallas Counties. Therefore, it was necessary to educate the men and women around the issues of a healthy lifestyle. Empowering our citizens by giving them the information that they need to take back their communities was the ultimate goal.

In total, the adult leadership program ran for about a year. Initially, we got off to a rocky start, and unfortunately, we were never really able to recover. Getting people to show up for the meetings was the easy part. Also, for the most part, all of the individuals who participated recognized and respected the different backgrounds represented in the program. Everyone was respected and those involved were given an opportunity to express themselves. These were the positive results. However, when it came down to deciding what project we would implement in our county, they could not decide. Ultimately, I believe this was the result of implicit and indirect racial tensions. There were great needs in the African American areas; on the other hand, it seemed that the white members of the group felt that we didn't need to go there unless we had something to place in a Caucasian community as well. That simply was not feasible. It was not possible for us to do so much with so few resources, and because of this, the project began falling apart.

In the end, we just could not meet on common ground. Needless to say, we were unable to implement a project. There were other issues that the group could have tackled, but they could not agree on one specific thing to do. Again, it mostly came down to a fruitless pursuit of balance: if we did something in the black communities, we needed to do it in the white communities as well. If we did something for public schools, we also had to do it for private ones. At the conclusion of the program, I didn't feel that it was my responsibility to select a project to fund that a majority of the group members didn't support. I wasn't going to do a project that only I was invested in. Instead, I was willing to back away from my own ideas, and ask what else could be done. Still, we never got around the deadlock. So, being a member of the financial team for the grantor, I said that it was in the best interest of the program to refund the money because the course hadn't decided on a project. In the end, the brinkmanship of some group members brought down the entire capacity of the program, resulting in little visible change in the community.

Reflections

Despite these shortcomings, the mere fact that these adults were able to meet, set aside their racial differences, and talk about community issues for about a year was, without question, a positive takeaway. I often ask myself if I would do anything differently if I were given the chance to do the entire program over again, and I have decided that I wouldn't. As both a student and the program's coordinator, I had only one vote. Had others decided on a project and gotten the majority of votes, I would have agreed to it, even though I wasn't in that majority and wouldn't be getting what I had initially wanted. I was willing to accept that. Still, although I wouldn't change anything about my approach to the program, I had a bad feeling after it finished. About the same time that the adult course was happening, I had a youth leadership program that was running simultaneously. This experience was surprisingly different. Even though they faced similar challenges, those involved in the youth program overcame them, but in the adult course, the participants could not surpass the obstacle of deadlock.

In view of my experience with both adult and youth leadership programs, it becomes clear to me that the experience of the latter was a profound turning point in my life. The relative lack of success with the adult course surprised me. All of our meetings went smoothly, and even the planning process seemed to lead in the right direction. In my eyes, everyone recognized each other's individuality and role in the community. Yet when it boiled down, we weren't able to work together. This was disappointing for me because I enjoy working with adults. However, as an Extension coordinator, it is more practical to mold, shape, and inform children. Their education will better our collective future, and with the right information, they can create positive changes. That's what I like to do: create growth in the community. And oftentimes, change equates with growth.

Nevertheless, I don't regret any of the time spent in the adult leadership program. I learned a lot from the process, and most of this involved the simple lesson that we don't always win. We can work hard, meet and greet, do everything on the agenda, but at the end of the day, our programs can result in failure. That's challenging. It is disheartening because you think you're getting somewhere. I thought we were. When change wasn't implemented, I was dissatisfied.

As a result, this experience taught me that there is still a lot of work to be done. We can work together every day and go home at night, relieved that that's over. Then we have to do it all over again the next month. If that's the case, then our community has a major problem on its hands. We're going to have to try to find a way of getting our citizens to grasp the concept that if they want change, they have to want to be a part of that process. If we come to the table of deliberation wearing masks of feigned cooperation, only to remove them at night when the meetings are over, change will never reach us. I think that is what's happening in Perry County, and it hinders the progress of our community.

As I reflect on my role as coordinator, I've learned that every day, from start to finish, I need to give 100 percent to whatever it is I'm doing. I need to be committed. If I expect citizens to buy into what I'm teaching, they first need to see that I'm committed to the process, too. Dedication from our local citizens has been a problem. Many will commit momentarily, but then say that it's getting old. Despite this sentiment, we have to know that if we want to change anything for the better, it's going to take devotion to the cause. We need focus from everyone involved, whether it's individuals, institutions, or agencies. We all need to play a part.

From my experience, commitment often takes shape in the form of persistence. It's rare that I will accept "no" for an answer. If I can't get a program done in one place, I'll move it to another. I will always continue to try until I get the job done. When I feel like I'm meant to accomplish something, I drive to fulfill that goal. That's the important lesson that I've gained from my work: to not accept "no" for an answer. If I feel passionate about something I'm going to find a way. Consequently, I've experienced some powerful steps forward in the community. Regarding youth leadership, I've gotten additional funds now from an agency that I thought would not give me anything more than what they provided in the past. Also, when people call to say, "Keep it up," and "We want you to be a part of our program," that lets me know that I'm doing the work I should be doing.

Since I accepted the position of Extension coordinator, I've gained a lot of experience. What it has taught me is that the men and women who serve in this role are in a unique position. In Alabama, there are 67 counties, and each one has an Extension office. How many other agencies can say that they have that type of presence? I like to imagine what would happen if all of our employees were out in the field, committed to the communities they worked for. The impact that Extension could have on this state would be enormous. As professionals in this line of work, we have a duty: our mission states that we are here to enhance quality of life. Contrary to some misconceptions, we don't make things up and just say, "Oh, let's try something new today!" People recognize Extension as being a part of a land-grant institution that disperses relevant, research-based information. Therefore, if all we do is sit in our offices and we don't get out into the communities themselves, then we are doing a disservice to those around us.

Ultimately, the hardest part of my job is dealing with the issue of having knowledge, but struggling to integrate it with the day-to-day lives of citizens in my county. Many times, people are altogether unaware of the services that we provide. I was in a meeting once, and a young lady from the Department of Children's Health was there. She was speaking, and she said that Cooperative Extension was the best-kept secret in Alabama. She began naming various programs that Extension provides for the community that she had previously been unaware of because she was in a state-level position. When she traveled across Alabama, she was hearing what was going on from everyday people, and they brought up Extension almost every time. This is why we need to find a way to let the public know what we can provide.

For the most part, a majority of our county's citizens are caught in the web of this economic downturn. Community development is what Extension is about today. As a whole, the men and women working in Extension need to continue developing new methods of getting to where the community actually needs us. I'm not sure how we can reach this point, but it's going to be a challenge for us to survive in the future if we can't meet the needs of the citizens. If we cannot be a resource for the public's future growth, then it may result in the downward spiral of Extension as an institution. We're going to have to find a way to change that.

Interview conducted by Theodore R. Alter

Elevating the Conversation

A Profile of Bill McGowan
Community Development Educator, Sussex County Extension Office
University of Delaware Cooperative Extension

While he admits that people "drive me crazy at times," Bill McGowan tells us in this profile that he has "an unfailing faith in the human race." As we see when we read the stories about his work, his faith is active rather than passive. He pursues it with a fierce commitment to build understanding and respect across lay and professional lines. Against the odds, and against the grain of cultures and practices in many sectors, he shows us how deliberative processes can be used in Extension (and other professions) to "elevate the conversation" beyond technical matters in complex and heated environmental regulation challenges to make room for citizens' values and interests. Making it more rather than less useful, the story he tells about his use of deliberative processes in Delaware is not mainly a success story. It's full of setbacks, ambiguities, and uncertainties. Because of these qualities, it reads and feels more like a conversation with a friend over a drink than it does a polished and tidy case study.

My name is Bill McGowan and I am a community development educator in Sussex County Delaware with Delaware Cooperative Extension. I still use the old title, county agent. I carry around the Norman Rockwell painting of a county agent and if folks ask me what I do I say, "Do you recognize this fellow in this picture?" I say, "Yes, I am a county agent."

Norman Rockwell Visits a County Agent by **Norman Rockwell (Illustration provided by Curtis Licensing)**

I tell people that I have worked for the University of Delaware for 20 years and that I have changed my job several times at the university. I jokingly tell folks that if I want to change my job, I get new business cards. I put a job title on the business card and if nobody picks up on it in six months, then it is my new job. That has been fairly successful so far!

I got into community development in 1989. I was hired as a water quality assistant. Basically, that came about because I walked into the office and I said to the county agent that was there (he was the county agent that I used when I was a farm supply manager in Laurel), "Derby, you need any help?" He said, "Yeah if you're willing to work for 10 bucks an hour." I said, "At this point in time, I am." So I did. I came onboard as the water quality assistant working with five growers. It was an externally funded project. I worked in water quality for the early years of my career. The issues that come about with water quality in Sussex County are complex issues—real community development work. Somewhere around 2000, I adopted community development as my job title. And I'm still here!

I was born in Wilmington, Delaware, and grew up in the suburbs. I'm the oldest of seven kids: myself, a brother, four sisters and a younger brother. Delaware is a small state, and less than half the population are native Delawareans. I have this crazy attachment for Delaware. Jefferson

106

called it the Diamond State. It's a jewel among states. However, what we do in this state drives me crazy. But I still think we are a jewel. I still think we are a special place, but we just do not know it.

Growing up, I enjoyed it. I have been blessed, as I said, as the oldest of seven kids. We all still get along. We all have fun. We enjoy each other. We just had our second reunion this summer and we don't do it often enough.

We lived in Wilmington for four years. When I was four, we moved into one of the earliest suburbs north of Wilmington. All that area up north now, except for what is called the Brandywine Valley, is suburbs. It's built up. It's gone. There are at least 1,200 people up there per square mile. You cannot find a piece of open space or rolling open space that is not county park land or land that literally is what we call chateau country, preserved by the large estates of the DuPonts. I grew up in a fairly typical suburb. It was a quarter-acre lot, but heck, I got to play capture the flag, I had a creek I could fall into and not drown, I had green space, I had sidewalks. It was good.

I think between high school and grade school and a little stint in the seminary, I've got 12, 13 years of Catholic education. That's kind of scary! I went to Salesianum, which is a Catholic high school, all male, in Wilmington. It's where my dad went. Dad graduated in 1942. One of my teachers, Father Bob Kenney, was his classmate. Right out of Sallies I joined the priesthood. That's how it was done at the time. Right after high school, off you went to the novitiate. "Goodbye mom, goodbye dad, I guess I'll see you sometime!" It was a yearlong immersion into the Oblates of St. Francis de Sales. The novitiate was actually on a farm in Childs, a little crossroad just west of Elkton, Maryland. I spent the next year-and-a-half as a novice on a farm in rural Maryland. It was my first pretty good dose of agriculture and I could never shake that. It was just a wonderful, wonderful experience. I stayed in the Order for two and a half years.

I guess the earliest mentor I had, who was particularly influential, was Father Bill Keech. Thinking back it was Father Keech who inspired me to enter the seminary. He was a low-key, wonderful individual, very caring; made sure you had your head on straight. Last year I got a call that the class of 1964 was putting together a scholarship fund honoring Bill Keech. From just an immediate call-around they ended up with a $25,000-dollar pledge, picking up the phone one time. Father Keech is just a spiritual, quiet, fun-loving individual.

I was in the school shows led by Father Keech and a colleague. It was classic yin and yang, with Fr. Bill as the yin. His partner was a very hard taskmaster. As the director, orchestra conductor, etc., he brooked no nonsense. Then, of course, there was Father Keech. He was in charge of back stage, the set, and the stage crew. He was the support guy—the nurturer.

I see myself as an intuitive person. On Myers-Briggs tests I tend to fall in the category of healer and wise person, but still questioning my life journey. That is what it is. This life is a journey and we have to figure out ultimately what we were meant to do in this world. Well, I'm still trying to figure it out.

I guess as I go through life, I would say Father Keech was the guy who literally started me on my life's path. It was because of the way he lived his life. I sensed there was a goodness in this man, and that's why I joined the Oblates—to walk the path he was on. The Oblate experience exposed me to agriculture! Nothing like culling the layer house on the hottest day of summer. . . .

I continued along this line of service to one another. It is about people. The other person, when I think about influential mentors, is Jay Windsor. Jay was the ornamental horticulture agent and County Director. He would give you the shirt off his back. He's just rock solid. He was there for you. He gave you a lot of leeway to get things done.

So these are people who I know and respect. Hopefully I internalize who they are, and they are now part of who I am.

After the Oblates I enrolled in plant science at the University of Delaware. More roots stuff. This notion of being in agriculture and this notion of helping people have always been part of my makeup, of who I am. If you look at my career, I have done several different things. I framed houses while in college. I got out of college and continued in the construction business, and had a small business with a buddy. It was called Master Construction. We did porches, roofs, and additions, all that good stuff.

All of a sudden, I said, "Whoa, whoa, I need to get back into ag," and I became the farrowing house manager for a swine operation on the eastern shore of Maryland. This was my first introduction to factory farming. I could not believe this place! I lasted nine months. It was industrialized agriculture right from the get-go. It was the only location of that size on the eastern shore of Maryland. It was down in Federalsburg. I was the fastest teeth and tails cutter and castrator on the entire eastern shore of Maryland. I had 240 sows under roof at one time, 30 sows farrowed every 4 and a half days. I averaged nine pigs per litter. I had 4 houses, 30 sows on each end of the house split in half, so 240 under one roof. That was my introduction, until I said, "Get me the hell out of here!" I went to work for Southern States, which is a farm supply cooperative. I spent eight years with them, and that is how I got down to Sussex County.

I was a manager of farm supplies for Southern States down here for four years. It's where I met the county agent that I talked about earlier, Derby Walker. Within Southern States, I enjoyed the sales and the service, but mostly the service. I had this mind-set for all the time I worked with Southern States that it was kind of like helping people—get the crops planted, get them the fertilizer, get them the pesticides they need, move, move, move, go, go, go, help these guys get the best crop they can with the best service.

Then I worked for Coastal Nurseries for four years. We had field-grown nursery, a retail garden center, and a commercial and residential landscaping business. I did that for four years and then left for the University of Delaware.

I guess those are the threads there. These notions of agriculture—of being outdoors, of service, of helping people—are what got me to where I am. I am a county agent. Wow, what a job. Derby was the old-time county agent model. He was a consultant when I came on board. Derby had the office next door to me, and Derby had his clientele. I was supposed to be the water quality/ag agent, but while Derby was handling his clientele, I was pretty much running around with a groundwater flow model. I was not doing the ag troubleshooting stuff, and I knew fairly early in my career that the ag agent model I knew professionally was not going to be the agent that we need for the issues that Extension is going to address in the future.

With that knowledge, I went back to school and picked up a master's in adult education. Reading guys like Brookfield, Mezirow, Horton, and Freire, they resonated with me. I just sensed that this is what is needed. I was running into water quality issues, land-use stuff, and people shouting at each other, and you know you're not going to deal with that just by going out on a farm and saying, "Well okay, but you know, integrated pest management." It was much more complex. We had to learn to talk to each other about stuff. That was in the early 1990s. I have never looked back.

I learn by doing. I've done collaborative problem solving, but when I read Ron Hustedde's *Community Issues Gathering*, I was sitting there going, "Ah, this looks pretty good to me. This is something important." Around that time, the University of Delaware Continuing Education became one of the public policy institutes (PPI) for the Kettering Foundation, and I joined almost immediately. I said, "Okay, I need to be on this board." Since 1994, we've kept that title in our affiliation with Kettering.

I hate to say there have not been any particular situations that were impactful on my path. I hate to be so boring, but I am a composite of who I am. I have made changes. I have changed within the university, within the paradigm. I have been privileged. I have had 20 years to grow and change my job and do what I do. Leaving the Oblates, and I do not want to go all the way back there, but you know, that was a big deal. I took vows of chastity, poverty, and obedience, and this was back in a very tumultuous time in the church. Vatican II was in 1964. I joined in 1968, and I left in 1971.

Leaving the nursery was hard because of John, the guy I went to work for in the nursery. I had left Southern States and went to work at that nursery because he and I were best friends in college. He was a really good guy, a rock-solid guy. He took a chance on that nursery and he took a chance on me going in as his wholesale nursery manager. I needed a change in my job so I did a stint working in the nursery, and crawled around and dug plants and all that kind of stuff. But I got bored. I took the bids for commercial landscape and I ran some of the commercial landscaping crew. Ultimately I had to leave, because the nursery was in hard times. I look back and I think I was responsible for some of those hard times, because I was responsible for things I was not good at. I was not a good manager or detail person, and that was hard for me when I had to tell John, "I have to go." I look back on it now and I wonder. The nursery failed, and I do not know if it was because of undercapitalization or things like that, but I look back and wonder if that was partly because of me. So there are things that I look back on and say, "Wow." I do not want to be that person that just kind of walks through life, and once you walk past something you leave a wreck in your wake and it was you who did it, but you are just kind of blissfully walking on down the road. I really do not want to be that person. I will tell you that, but I have seen it happen with others.

The Inland Bays Project

The story I'm going to share deals with pollution control strategies. This was a seminal event for me in my Extension work. This is when I really had to start thinking if this deliberative stuff works, and what I want to do with it. I'm prefacing with that now because I do not use the words *public choices*, and I had never really adopted it as a classic Extension model. But everything I have done, probably since 2000 or 2001, has usually had some piece of deliberation embedded into it. Whether we frame an issue, whether we are doing work for the forestry service or the nature conservancy or Delaware's Department of Natural Resources and Environmental Control (DNREC) or whatever, I have embedded deliberation into it.

A quick overview: The Environmental Protection Agency (EPA) was threatened for not forcing Delaware to meet the standards of the Clean Water Act. The EPA in a settlement with the state basically said, "Okay Delaware, you need to establish Total Maximum Daily Loads (TMDL's) for all your impaired watersheds." TMDL's are loading rates for whatever is impairing your water: nitrogen, phosphorus undissolved oxygen, or that kind of stuff. Well, God bless Delaware! Since we have been around for so long, 85 to 90 percent of our waters are impaired. So time to start picking watersheds, and it happens they picked the Inland Bays, which is the most impaired watershed. Delaware not only said in their agreement that we will establish TMDL's, but we will establish pollution control strategies (PCS) that will tell us how to reach the TMDL's.

This was about 1999. Prior to that, because of my water quality work, I sat on the citizens' advisory committee for the Inland Bays. The history of the Bays is long in Delaware, as far as environmental policy goes. We had Governor Castle appoint the Inland Bays monitoring committee. We spent five years planning on how to deal with the pollution in the Inland Bays. That work finished in 1989, and somebody said, "Hey look, we can become a national estuary program." Delaware, not being stupid, decided to take the money, and we went into another five-year planning process to develop a comprehensive conservation management plan (CCMP) for the Inland Bays. That was facilitated by the EPA and the DNREC. I sat through five years of that process, resulting in the national estuary program CCMP. By the end I was actually the chair of the citizens' advisory committee. I was one of the signatories of the legislation that created the Center for the Inland Bays in 1994. The center would be responsible for the implementation of the CCMP.

It's interesting when you go back to this stuff. I was sitting through a facilitated process and watching how this thing went. Meanwhile, I was taking my master's courses. Seeing a professional facilitator work through things was interesting. It was learn-as-you-go. Long story short, that was my affiliation with the Inland Bays.

Back to the story. As DNREC was gearing up to work on the PCS in 1999, the Center for the Inland Bays had created what they call tributary action teams to work on the three bays: the Indian River, the Rehoboth, and Little Assawoman Bay. DNREC was starting a separate process, forming a committee to do the TMDL's. It seemed to me there were two parallel processes: the Center for the Inland Bays' action teams were getting ready to start talking about the Inland Bays, and then you had DNREC starting to bring together a whole bunch of people to start talking about pollution control strategies. Why have two tracks?

It surfaced fairly early that the Center for the Inland Bays was ready to go. Their outreach and education coordinator, Ed, is a great guy. He had just started to work for the Center for the Inland Bays, maybe two or three years previously. He's a native Delawarean with a degree in marine policy/marine science. He was previously a naturalist at Trap Pond State Park. So here he is doing his good work. Ed was crazy enough to start thinking about how to develop strategies for pollution in the Inland Bays. Another fellow, Joe, worked for the Sea-Grant Marine Advisory Service. I had worked with Joe a couple of times before actually teaching a course together with several other folks on collaborative problem solving. Joe, because of his sea grant side, was very interested in facilitative processes. We all somehow came up with the idea of, "Let's see if we can get this thing done."

We convinced DNREC to allow us to merge the processes. Now, that was pretty cool. They said, "Okay we will do the TMDL's, but you do the pollution control strategies in this watershed." Ed held this meeting, and we got everybody on board. We started out with three tributary action teams working on their bays to figure out pollution control strategies. We did it the fairly standard way: here is your committee, we need to get educated on what the issue is, we will develop recommendations, and then we will go out and inform folks about what we did. That is how we started.

We did the education, we took a bus trip, and we did this and did that. Now remember, we have three different action teams going on here, three different bays. Technically, the stuff is supposed to be different in three of the watersheds, but not really.

Something happened where it just was not working, and I do not know what it was—divine inspiration or whatever—but I said, "This is not working. We're going to have to do something different." That's when I started to talk to Joe and Ed about framing the issue and getting the teams to frame the issues so their friends and neighbors could talk about it, and then we will go ahead and see where that takes us. That was the start of it. (And of course you will always hear us reference a few black and tans!)

There were probably several sessions that were informal sessions. Joe brought the reality check. Joe wants the data. He wants to know: How are people going to make decisions? Where is the information they need to make decisions upon? Ed was the driver. Ed was the organizer. I did not want to be bothered with calling people and doing all the arranging, but Ed was willing to let Joe and me engage in these conversations. He was the logistics guy. He kept us on track!

The Center for the Inland Bays was responsible for pulling this stuff off. Joe and I were the guys who stood up in front of people and tried to get them to do things. So it took a while and I thought it was helpful, because I tend to be somewhat naïve and just kind of figure that it will work. It works. It makes sense. You just put people in a room and you frame it in a way that surfaces their values, and they will immediately go into conversation and we will get things done. It will be okay. Well, Joe and Ed were not buying that at all. I mean Joe's going, "Where's the data? How are they going to make decisions?" Joe had done some stuff with citizen juries and he comes from a mediation background.

First lesson learned was that it was very, very, hard for the folks on the teams, who were geared to solving a problem in a certain way, to change gears. I practically had to whack them with a two-by-four. I had to tell them, "Nope. Done. We are not solving the problem anymore. It's over. No more. *No mas.*" So literally, to be able to move them from a problem-solving piece to an issue-framing thing, that was very difficult. But they got it. They finally got it.

I learned a second lesson from this experience. I started my framing with the question, "What should we do?" Dumb, dumb, dumb. No, it's not dumb; it's lessons learned. I never did that again, because to move to values after listing all of the action pieces was extremely difficult. Instead, I start with the questions, "What are your concerns? What is really important to you?" We spent some time working through pulling it out, disseminating what people were really trying to say. What was behind that action item? And so I was missing a step there.

There were some other issues with DNREC. They would let us move forward on one side, but internally DNREC was developing their own pollution control strategies in another program called Whole Basin. They were developing a comprehensive plan to manage the Inland Bays water-shed, and we found out about this. I'm going, "Are you kidding me? What, what are you doing?" We had meetings with DNREC saying, "You cannot do this. You straighten the hell up!" And, actually, they said, "Okay fine, we understand." We had a meeting with our tributary action teams and DNREC's Whole Basin team and said, "Okay what is going on here?" We got that settled; they allowed us to move forward. They agreed to start writing fact sheets about the information we would need further on down the road on septic systems, land use, zoning, and things like that. We went forward with the public process, saying "Let's listen to our friends and neighbors."

So we had three tributary action teams framing their issues. One of the tougher members of a team was a farmer. He was just, "Show me the data, show me the data, show me the data." This is all about nonpoint source pollution. The Inland Bays watershed is supplied by groundwater, recharged by rainfall. So you can't point a finger at the cause of the pollu-tion: it's nonpoint pollution. So this guy is hammering away on the science. By the way, we were using the model that the National Issues Forums (NIF) promotes for developing what are called "issue guides" that center on a framed public issue, with three distinct choices for how to deal with the issue spelled out. In this case, we ultimately had a choice that said, "Science and Cents." (We were fairly cute in this thing—cents: C E N T S.)

So we had three watersheds. Ultimately, we had to go out and have these forums and it kind of occurred to us that, with the similarity between the three watersheds, there was really no major distinction. So we put the three teams together and said, "Guys, we really would like to merge your issues." I think we had been successful in building trust with them, because they heard us and they allowed us to play with it.

We ended up developing a single issue guide for all three watersheds. And I actually think I shipped it to one of the folks who did some of the early framing of issues for Kettering. They may have done the first issue framing book, *How You Frame an Issue*. I shipped it out to them for a review and they gave us some insights. One of the choices that stayed in was Science and Cents, because it showed up in different themes throughout the other issue books. We kept it in there and off we went. That is the story. We went out, we had five forums, folks came, had some good conversations, and came up with a couple of building blocks for future work. There were a lot of logistical pieces that we could have done much better.

Let me tell you about the forums. I do not mind contentious situations. I just do not mind, because I truly believe in the forum process. Here are ground rules: you are all big people; this is an opportunity for you to interact as big people; and I am here to kind of help you do that. That is what they did. They went through the choices. They had conversations. There were perspectives from the agricultural community: "Don't take away my land rights," and "Don't blame it all on me."

I think there is a mystique around deliberation. You know, when does it happen? Well honest to God, you better be ready. You would have to do what you are doing now: tape every forum, and try and find out where that deliberative spot was, because it comes and it goes so quickly that if you can't capture it, you miss it. You have to be able to tap it. When we finally peeled the onion we thought about the themes that came out of the conversation. We did a pre- and a post-analysis of what folks were doing, we took notes, and I think we used the notes to help us think about what was going on.

The biggest thing for me was that we elevated the conversation from a strictly "let's reduce the nutrients" conversation to a much broader issue. One of the recommendations I really, really enjoyed, and thought was strong, was concurrency between governments. That came out. It's a "don't tell me what to do when the city of Lewes can do this or the city of Rehoboth can do this, and the state of Delaware is doing this, and you don't even have your ducks in a row, so don't be telling me what to do." So concurrency was a big one. Of course, other stuff came out, like fairness. People were willing to discuss the notion of taxes, saying, "Don't tax us." Well people are willing to pay taxes sometimes. This showed up in a meeting. They are willing to pay something if they know there is something else to be gained by that. But they want to know specifics. They want to know where their money is going, and that informed where we went. That allowed us to create a broader spectrum to have a discussion around the nitrogen, phosphorus, and other materials. They literally became the principles for the more specific pollution control strategies that evolved over the next year.

What are the outcomes, and where does it stand today? I'm a little fuzzy on times, but this should be close. We had the forums and, shortly after, brought all interested forum participants back together. I think it was a two-day meeting where we developed a first cut of the PCS. We submitted the draft to DNREC for comment. DNREC made comments on where the PCS needed work. We then spent a year working with citizens' groups through the issues—nitrogen reduction from septic systems, concurrency, pieces like that revising the PCS. This was where the fact sheets from the DNREC's Whole Basin team came in. We then submitted that to DNREC. A team continued to work on storm water regulations. I was no longer engaged with the tributary teams at this point. With the final submittal of recommendations to DNREC the tributary teams disbanded. Unfortunately, and this is what I see as a major failure, DNREC became a black hole. The recommendations from what I understand went into an internal review and reappeared about three or four years later. When the PCS resurfaced, it was at an official workshop and hearing to "promulgate pollution control strategy regulations within the bay's watershed."

Well then, all the good will and all the public input was gone. There was no continuity between a very public process and what was now happening. There were people who had left. People did not stay connected to the process. The development community, who had sat at the table earlier and had a voice and input in septic regulations and more, came back with a vengeance. For example, one of the promulgations was buffer strips around farm fields. In this county, any farm field is zoned "ag residential," which allows two units per acre. If you take away the ability to build on land now identified as a buffer you are taking away lots. The development community rose up in the typical Delaware fashion and went to the legislators— threatened to do this, threatened to do that. DNREC pulled the promulgation and went into a year-long meeting with the development community to hear "their side's" concerns, and things like that.

The DNREC, in their alleged settlement with the development community, as far as I am concerned, gave away the store. They pulled off the stops on the buffers. The Center for the Inland Bays, with Ed now the director, had the courage and the scientific evidence to tell DNREC they were wrong. The DNREC stepped back and revisited their recommendation or their settlement with the development community, and they then had the courage to admit they were wrong. They toughened their buffer stance, and the regulations are now promulgated. There is a lawsuit. The county is suing DNREC over the way the language reads in the promulgation. That is where we are: in a lawsuit.

Reflections

I think this whole thing was rewarding, but I would think the most rewarding aspect was working with Joe and Ed, helping them understand, and working and learning as a team. Not to be remiss but we had another team member, Kathy, who was on loan from DNREC. Kathy was working on her PhD in the College of Marine Science at the University of Delaware with a focus on how to make policy. She was asking questions and helping us learn. It was a great team that would not let any of us get away with anything. I had to be passionate and think a little deeper.

I learned things. Do not start with action steps. I learned that sometimes I become an advocate for citizens with public agencies because public agencies know they have to engage the public, but they do not know how to do it. Sometimes they will just look for any tool to check the public involvement box. One of my concerns was that deliberation sounds pretty cool. Public talk, real choices, it is the way to do this. But is it just checking the public box? Is it just saying, "Well we did it, we engaged them" and then just moving on? To me, there are more steps in the process. If a public agency is going to use this, are they really willing to listen, to take the extra steps that an engaged public will ask for? Are they really willing to step up? DNREC did, they really did. To have that access and to have the willingness of that agency to allow us to move forward was incredible if you think about it. It was a learning environment. This was a "learn as you go" thing. We were trying things out and the regulatory agency that had a lot to lose was literally allowing us to do that.

When I say advocate for public people, you do not want folks to get shuffled into a check-the-box public process. You had the meeting, check the box, let's move on. I do not want that to happen.

The whole process was rewarding, because it works. If folks can engage an issue and if they can wrestle with it, then they can look at trade-offs, they are willing to spend time night after night after night trying to do what is right. You cannot ask for more than that. If you go back to where we started, and this is all about Extension, that is what we do. To me, that is what we are about. This happened to be one instance that was linear enough that there is a story to tell about it, and so that is why I picked it.

I think the citizens involved in this process got it. We had this highly educated blueberry farmer who was the Science and Cents guy. Tom, God rest his soul, Tom would just keep pounding away on this science and cents stuff. We had a 5,000-acre farmer, Dickey. He hung in on the whole thing. He was there right from the beginning. Gave a tour of the farm and the vertically integrated poultry industry for whom he worked. That was a real eye opener for those who have never seen a farm. We had others, town managers, citizens, all kinds.

I'm recalling the framing piece, and here is the other major lesson for me. It is the framing. If you start at the beginning and you put crazy (I use the term loosely) people in a room and say we have to frame the issue for your friends and neighbors to talk about, there is more learning done, more deliberation done in that framing session than sometimes you'll hear in those two hours at a public meeting.

Going back to Kettering, in one of my early years with the crew out there, they really did not want to talk about framing. I am sitting there going no, no, no, no. It is the framing piece. I really was not worried about the issue books with Kettering. I was worried that we would not get real issues back into the community and get these things framed up, and let's have a conversation about that stuff. Big take away for me was getting the people in the room, getting the thing framed, with people like Wolfgang and Dickey and Marian. All these people are busy people, and sitting in a room working through the question, "how are our friends and neighbors going to talk about this?" Then they can come into the forums, and they'll chime in, the whole deal.

It's interesting to think about other lessons from this experience. I mean, here I am, I have been working with Extension for 20 years. Early on, I read a book by Paulo Freire and Miles Horton. It is called *We Make the Road by Walking*. I think that title *We Make the Road by Walking* comes from a poem, but I just like the way it fits. *We Make the Road by Walking,* I believe, means there is no road and you need to do something, and when you are doing something, you are making the road. So I have never really had a formal program. I always feel organizationally challenged. "Well geez, I need some master gardeners. I got to be doing workshops. I got to be doing fact sheets." You know it is just kind of scary because these are things that you can check a box and measure. How many workshops? How many fact sheets? How many this and that? I am a little shaky when it comes to that. I mean I can tell you that I do strategic planning, I do facilitation, I do crisis management, I do a lot of that stuff. But try to summarize that into a program, and it gets a little difficult.

I'm working on something now called Heart and Soul, and I'm attempting to engage this county or the residents of this county in starting to think about who they are, what they want to be when they grow up. We have no land-use policy. We have no economic development strategy. We are a very mixed-bag county. I do not want to get into demographics, but I guess, and we all know this, you just continue to evolve. I tend to go where I need to be. I did not want to be in economic development, but I am in economic development now. I use what I learn as I grow. They always say to put it in the suitcase, you know, you have the tools, but I do not really look at deliberation as a tool. I look at it more as part of me. It's a process. I know you do not want to talk about it as a process, but I will wiggle it in there. I have framed some really weird things just so folks have an opportunity to talk about it.

Another lesson is to have faith in your public agencies. I don't mean that to be taken the wrong way. A lot of times we think that they are impediments and blockers, but what I have found is sometimes they just don't know. These people in the agencies are trained, they are just like us. They are trained in a technical field, and all of the sudden these are mid-managers that have to go out there and engage the public that, more than likely, is usually pissed off. We jokingly say around here the best way to get people to a meeting is to go out and stick red flags in their yard that says Department of Transportation. Then they show up at the meeting because they figure something is going to happen to their yard.

You have folks in planning with their literature that says yeah, involve the public. I have seen some of the public administration literature that only says better learn to engage your public. There are good people trying to get something done in a meaningful way. This whole public piece, particularly with the environment, is out there now. Anytime a public agency tries to go engage with the public they are setting them up to get people to take shots. Over my career I have set myself as the principle facilitator so the agency folk do not get gored. I'm there so the public agency can have a conversation with the public in a way that is not offensive. That is kind of a facilitator role, but it is part of it that with these agencies, there is a relationship there that can be built upon.

I have an unfailing faith in the human race although they drive me crazy at times! I find these events in many ways refreshing and reassuring, and I think other people do also. I want this to be in my work and I do not want to be quoting other people, but I mean if you create the condition and the environment, folks will talk to each other. I think many times that two hours on a forum is quite artificial. It's the beginning of a conversation. That is a lesson learned also. If folks could give us two hours a night for five nights they might have been able to get you some more, but two hours or three hours a night for one forum to cover three approaches, you are just dancing in the water. You are stirring the pot. You are baiting the hook for a deeper conversation, which they will have.

I think forums allow people to respect each other. They will give each other time and they will admit they are wrong, or that they have changed their opinion. I have seen that happen, and that is refreshing. But the YouTube of the whacko that started the ugly town meetings—the video with our congressman stunned by the woman standing up questioning Barack Obama's birth place—also happened in this county. We were so proud. We were so very, very proud. . . . Not!

This experience with the bay project and the deliberative work connects with my thoughts about Cooperative Extension. I am scared to death, very scared about the history of Cooperative Extension. No, not the history. I like the history, and I know there are spots of that history that I probably do not like, but I like our roots. I am scared of our future. I had the privilege of being on Extension's national Policy and Organizational Development Committee (PODC). I proposed to PODC that we should frame the issue of what the future of Cooperative Extension is, and have that deliberated at Extension's second national Galaxy Conference. That was in 2001, and they disbanded PODC about a year later. This continued demise of who we are at the administrative level—we have no sense of who we are. We have no sense of identity. We have very good people, but if you asked my colleagues what it means to be in Extension, you are going to get about 50 or 60-some different answers.

On the national level, it's quite disheartening watching the disappearance of the Cooperative Extension System to CREES to NIFA. Fill in the acronyms because the names are so convoluted.

I think we in Extension have a lot to offer. I really do. Anytime I have an opportunity to speak to people, I usually start with "Does anybody know what I do for a living?" I will start with a county agent. Generationally that gets me Green Acres from one or two. If that doesn't work, I go with Cooperative Extension. That really loses them. I had 120 FFA kids the other day in four different classes and asked them that question. Does anybody know what a county agent is? What is Cooperative Extension? Very scary. Nobody knew. It was pretty spooky, and they were from farm backgrounds and urban backgrounds. When folks do not get Cooperative Extension they usually will get 4-H. Even some of these FFA kids did not get 4-H. Go figure. I don't think I'm imagining this, and I find it scary. We are a legend in our own mind. That one really scares me.

Earlier, I was digging around in some of my old papers and I found a letter that I never sent. I wrote it to our outgoing dean of the college, and he was the interim acting director for Extension. It was a pretty hard assessment of our system along the lines of what I just told you. We have no sense of identity. We do not know who we are. If you do not know who you are, and you do not know where you are going, how are you going to get there? I mean wow, what are we doing? I would say that translates to the national level.

What is Extension about? The quick one is to help people to put knowledge to work. But there's also the notion of public work, of helping a diverse group of people create things of lasting importance for their community and society. I think that is Extension work. I really do. To me, the root of Extension is working with a diverse group of people to create things of lasting importance. And you know, they do not realize that a lot of that stuff they are creating are things of lasting importance! If you have a conversation about your town and that conversation leads to doing something about your town, guess what you just did? You may have sparked something of lasting importance. So that to me is Extension work. Hopefully that's the work I do every day.

Interview conducted by Theodore R. Alter

Postscript—Bill McGowan was appointed the USDA Rural Development State Director for Delaware and Maryland in 2013. His picture of Norman Rockwell's *Norman Rockwell Visits a County Agent* hangs prominently on the wall and reminds him daily of why Extension work—public work—is so important.

Showing Up and Being There

A Profile of Daryl Buchholz
Associate Director (Ret.), Cooperative Extension
Kansas State University

Critics like Wendell Berry have long condemned agricultural Extension faculty, administrators, and county-based agents for being arrogant technocrats who advance their own career interests, and the interests of large multinational corporations, instead of the public's. As such, they could be seen as exemplars of an anti-democratic *rather than a democratic professionalism who have institutionalized—for more than a century in American higher education—a deeply damaging* misalignment *between institutional routines and citizens' work and values. In light of this charge, how surprising and refreshing it is to hear Daryl Buchholz's voice. It does not speak with a technocratic, corporate-serving arrogance, but reflects, instead, a democratic, public-minded humility. Telling us how important "showing up and being there and having a personal relationship" has been in his many years of Extension work in Missouri and Kansas, he reveals how and why he has been willing to engage in difficult conversations that reveal some of his own imperfections. What he says to farmers and others who don't work for universities, in a way that opens a path for deliberative public work that respects different forms and sources of knowledge, "I don't know. That sounds like a problem we need to work on, and maybe we work on it together."*

My name is Daryl Buchholz. I am associate director for the Cooperative Extension service at Kansas State University. My official title is Associate Director for Extension and Applied Research. The responsibilities are providing the day-to-day leadership role for Cooperative Extension, where my immediate supervisor is the dean of the College of Agriculture and director for the Cooperative Extension service and the agricultural experiment station. I have been in this position for just a little more than six years.

To give you a picture of Extension in Kansas, we have 265 local Extension positions across the state. We have 105 counties. We're actively engaged in organizing multicounty units or districts, which is made possible by an organizational structure and funding opportunity that was created by state statute. Currently we have about one-third of the counties in some kind of formal, multicounty relationship. It is a locally driven effort; that's the reason why all 105 counties are not organized in multicounty districts. They sort of happen with two counties coming together, one district at a time.

Currently about 225 to 230 of the 265 local Extension positions are filled. We have a certain number that are being held open. We also have some local funding situations that force counties to hold positions open, given the state of the economy. In addition to that, we have about 80 FTEs of faculty who have Cooperative Extension responsibilities across the College of Agriculture, College of Human Ecology, and the College of Engineering. With joint appointments, that probably equates to about 120 individuals who have formal assigned responsibility for Extension work.

The other snapshot I would give of Cooperative Extension at Kansas State is that while I say we have 120 faculty, we have a lot more than that who are engaged in various forms of proactive engagement—Extension-related work—from across the campus. That is an extremely positive culture of Kansas State University demonstrating commitment of faculty to serving the needs of the people in the state.

In terms of our budget, we have state and federal appropriated funds of roughly $25 million. We also have about $21 million in locally appropriated funds coming through counties or local districts. Grants and contracts make up another $13 to $14 million. So when you do the math and add all of that up, it is about a $57 million budget on an annual basis.

As with the nation, uncertainty is probably the name of the game in terms of budgetary stability. What we have experienced in recent years is that we have had some cutbacks in state funding. At the same time, our local funding has continued to show a small amount of growth, although uncertainty now resides as heavily with local funding and losing valuations at the local level, which is tightening that source of revenues. Kansas Extension has had fairly stable revenues with a small amount of growth over the years. Not extreme growth, but not extreme in terms of cutbacks either.

My journey to where I am today, as the associate director of Extension at Kansas State University, starts with my experience growing up on a farm in South Dakota. I am a native of South Dakota. I grew up on a small farm in the northeastern part of the state. Early on in my life I thought I was going to be an engineer, and I went off to college with that intent. It only took me a semester to decide my roots were tied more closely to agriculture and rural life.

My change in that direction was concerning to my parents at the time, because my dad had decided to take other work—he basically sold the assets of the farm. He kept the land, but sold off all the equipment and everything else, got out of farming, and started doing other things. Then I pick up the phone and called my dad to say, "I changed my major, I am now in agriculture." There was silence. "Don't worry, dad. I'm not coming back to farm." "Oh, okay!" I think he could see all of that in front of him. But it is agriculture; it is rural. That's where my roots are.

The farm I grew up on was very diversified. We had the cow/calf operation. We had all of the basic commodity crops of corn, wheat, grain sorghum, and alfalfa, and pasture land for grazing. We produced pretty much all of our own feedstock so that we could feed the livestock and grow them out and manage that whole process. It is a very diverse kind of a farming operation. Some of that has changed, but much still remains the same.

127

I always wanted to go to a land-grant university. I went to South Dakota State University in Brookings and did my undergraduate work there. I graduated with a degree in agronomy. I decided to take that route when I was between my sophomore and junior year. There was a research station that was close by home, where I lived, and I came home for the summers and would be looking for employment. I happened to get the opportunity to work on that research station.

I could see firsthand the research work that was going on and the importance of that work to that region of the state and its agricultural production. The manager of that research center and I got to visiting and I told him my interest is really in doing Extension. I was thinking about being an Extension agent and wanted to have his guidance in planning towards that goal. He said, "Why don't you continue on in your graduate work? You can do Extension work as a faculty member at some point in time." So I got more engaged in various kinds of research going on at that center. In my senior year, we arranged that I was going to do my graduate program under him at the research center in the summers and then I would go back to the campus and do my coursework.

In October of my senior year, he called me up and said, "Daryl, I'm moving to Oklahoma State University." He had worked out that he was going to have a graduate student stipend and he invited me to come down and work there, and I did. He had primarily an Extension appointment, so I did field-oriented research that had great applicability to Oklahoma agriculture, and specifically the wheat producers of Oklahoma. Then he guided me on to a PhD program, which I did here at Kansas State University with a major professor who had Extension responsibility. I did my field research work and completed that.

I have tried to figure out where the idea that I wanted to be an Extension agent came from. I think it is that I have always been an individual who takes pride in being able to help others. I think maybe my parents taught me that; I do not know. I felt it was sort of indigenous to myself. I thought about being a vo-ag teacher, or doing Extension work and working with the agricultural community. I felt like I could make a bigger contribution working in the agricultural community than being a vo-ag teacher in a classroom, and the classroom never excited me. I always had more of a desire to be in a much less formal setting than a regimented classroom.

I knew Extension when I was growing up on the farm. I was a 4-H kid. I grew up with the local 4-H club and did various kinds of projects with animals, horticulture, foods, and food preservation—all of the various kinds of projects. I learned public speaking in that arena, I learned some leadership skills, and I learned the importance of community service. So all of that, and being able to observe what Extension agents seemed to do from that vantage point, which is quite different from what they actually do as I look back! But I recognized that they have the opportunity to be a community leader.

My father did not have much of a relationship with Extension. We did through 4-H, but I think he used Extension in more of an indirect way of gathering the information. He was not very active with attending meetings, but he read a lot and he read a lot of things that were coming out of the university research and the Extension outreach programs.

To review, after receiving my undergraduate degree from South Dakota State University, I went for my master's at Oklahoma State and then did my PhD at Kansas State. I got all of my degrees one after another and all in agronomy. My expertise was soil fertility—nutrient management.

By the time I was finishing up my PhD, I was thinking about Extension in soil fertility. In my graduate defense—or in my prelims, I guess I would say—one of the faculty members asked the question, "Daryl, once we get you finished up through your PhD program, what is it that you would really like to do?" And I looked him square in the eye and I said, "I want your job!" He happened to be in Extension soil fertility and had responsibility for the soil-testing program in the state. I saw how he was engaged in both research and Extension education across the state—writing bulletins, doing the kinds of things that you could tell would be helpful to the agricultural producers in the state, and all that.

I guess I would say to my good fortune, as I was finishing up, a position had opened up at the University of Missouri, right next door, and it was to be the state Extension soil fertility specialist located in Columbia at the MU campus. It did not have a soil-testing program as a part of its responsibility, but it had all the other elements. I was fortunate enough that they offered me the position and I moved on over there and had almost 13 years of just fantastic work opportunity. Within a year after I arrived there, they asked me if I would take responsibility for the soil-testing program. I got the position and it was not too long before I came back here and said to my major professor, "I've got your job! It's just one state over."

I started my position at MU in 1980 and was there for almost 13 years. Through that, I was given the opportunity professionally to engage myself in leadership development. I think my administrators—department head, the dean, and the associate deans and all—saw some leadership capacity so they pushed me to participate in various types of leadership development activities. I would say those types of experiences are what really helped to broaden my perspective. Maybe to have a better understanding of what this whole Extension thing was really, truly all about.

When you ask someone, "What is it that you do as an Extension specialist?" invariably they will tell you, "Well, I'm the soil fertility Extension specialist," which does not tell you anything about what they do. That is probably the nature of the way I would have answered that at that time. It assumes that you understand what it means about you are actually doing.

When I first arrived in Missouri as the soil fertility Extension specialist, I had two major goals that I was working towards. Number one, the southern part of the state was seeing an increase in livestock production. It had a forage base that was not a very high quality, and they needed a higher quality forage base. One of the limiting factors was nutrients—nutrient management. So a great deal of my work was focused on helping the producers see the opportunities and understand the management techniques they needed to employ in order to improve the forage base in south Missouri, which would then improve the livestock systems. Number two was that the soil-testing program needed a complete overhaul in the state— to go back to everything we had in the way of recommendations and to reignite the interest that the producers had in knowing and understanding what the nutrient levels within their soil were, and what that meant for good management. I did that in my first several years.

I made a shift later on because of the whole element of conservation compliance. In north Missouri in the 1970s and early 1980s, they plowed up a lot of the hill ground to produce soybeans—very profitable and a highly erosive crop and production system. The USDA federal farm programs came along for conservation compliance and these northern Missouri farmers needed to figure out different cropping systems. They needed to figure out different ways of growing their crops, conserving their soil, and optimizing tillage and nutrient management. We had a team that helped transform the northern part of the state towards more conservation and no-till management. That consumed me for about four or five years— longer in terms of research, but with an active educational program.

It is difficult—but important—to provide a particular answer about what I do that actually represents what I really do. It is not just doing the soil expertise stuff. It is interacting with people in a learning process. It is a change process. It is understanding that here are all of the challenges and roadblocks that we see in front of us in order to achieve better productivity, in order to fulfill the federal programs on conservation compliance that said, "If you don't reduce your soil loss to a reasonable level in that area, federal benefits through the various farm programs would go away." You could not afford to farm without some of those kinds of benefits. It was to help producers understand what those roadblocks were that were coming, and maybe ways in which to either remove them or to get around them in some way, shape, or form. The engagement part of that was that I needed to understand the roadblocks.

We went out as a team and I sat in the back of the room and critically evaluated everybody else's presentations and thought about what I had said. When we would crawl back into the vehicle to head home, I told them,

"If I was an agricultural producer and I sat through that meeting, I wouldn't change a thing. All we did was stand up in front of that crowd and tell them what their problems are. They all know what their problems are. What they're looking for are solutions to those problems. We have got to reorient the way that we are approaching this whole thing, to help them address their problems. Not to hold up flags and say, 'This is going to be a problem if you go *this* route, this is going to be a problem if you go *that* route.'" Others felt that the status quo was the best they could do then. I said, "I don't believe that."

We made some changes. We reoriented the way in which we did our education to convince ourselves that a better management practice was towards no-till. We needed to show ways in which to alleviate all of the problems that we could envision in that no-till production system that they were going to encounter—new weed problems, new nutrient management problems, stand establishment problems, all of those kinds of things. I said, "We cannot just tell them that they are going to have those problems; we have to help these producers see how they can get through them."

It's a tough job, because in some cases, we did not have the answers yet. That forces you to go back into the literature. That forces you to go back into the field with your research and reorient some of your research work. We did research on both farms and experimental stations. We were doing on-farm field demonstration types of activities, and then we had more of the fundamental research going on in our research centers. It also meant that we were going to tackle new problems. Even with all of the things that we understood about a "clean-tilled, plowed soil system," I said. "It has problems, too. We know how to deal with them, so we don't consider them problems." We had to operate with that philosophy in this no-till system, so it took us a few years.

One of the other things that happened to me—and this was actually after I came back to Kansas State—is that I have a daughter who was in a sorority. She had a sorority event right here in the alumni center where we're talking today. I went to that sorority event on a Sunday afternoon, and this individual comes up to me and goes, "Were you ever at the University of Missouri?" I said, "Yeah." He told me what his name was. I said, "Your dad gave us the land to do research work up in northwest Missouri." I said, "It's memorialized to your dad, now." He said, "That's right." I said, "So whatever happened?" He said, "Daryl, there's a story that you never heard and that story is that when my dad did that and you guys agreed to come up and put plot work there that was devoted entirely to learning the management systems of no-till, and helping to teach us, we converted our entire farm to no-till that year."

I said, "I'm glad I didn't know that at the time. Knowing that would have scared me to death! We didn't have all of the answers." He said, "I knew you didn't have all the answers. But I knew the commitment that you had to finding those answers, and we figured we could just move right along with you." Then I said, "So how did it all work out?" He said, "We have not farmed in any other manner since then. We've done it all no-till, and it's all because of those plots. There's a lot more farmers up in that area that did exactly the same thing." I had never heard that story before. It is humbling to think that we had that kind of influence, but that is what Extension work really is.

In this work, gaining local trust is critical. I think that is the element that maybe we take for granted too much. We talk about how it takes time as an Extension professional to begin to develop an impact with an audience, and a part of all that is you have to build trust with that audience. They have to believe that you are working in their interest.

Obviously that is the way that gentleman felt, to have the confidence to convert—we were working on 25 acres and he was farming 1,600—all of that acreage into no-till, knowing full well that we did not have all the answers. But he trusted that we were going to be there in their interest, helping them sort through it and find a way even though he knew that their current systems were not working.

To build trust like that, you have to care. You have to care about those individuals that your work is going to benefit. You have to care to understand them. Now I think trust comes once they believe you under-stand. You show that you understand by being willing to engage in difficult conversation, and maybe displaying some of your imperfections in all of that. Being willing to say, "I don't know, that sounds like a problem we need to work on and maybe we work on it together." A lot of it includes just showing up and being there and having a personal relationship.

The Shift to Extension Administration

After spending almost 13 years in Missouri, my colleagues had con-vinced me that I could do administrative work, which is a trust relationship as well. I had been sort of the leader among our faculty that related in the crop production area. I had done that for probably half the time that I had been there, and they said, "Daryl, you've got those kinds of skills."

I received a phone call from a faculty member here at Kansas State. They said, "Daryl, there's a position here that I think you should come over and take a look at," which was to be the assistant director for ag and natural resources Extension. I took a look at it and I liked what I saw. They offered me the position and I came to Kansas State and did that for another 12 years before I stepped into the position of Associate Director of Extension and Applied Research.

Two years prior to my becoming the associate director, I was asked to fill in, on an interim basis, for the program leader responsibilities for 4-H youth development. It turns out that my work as 4-H program leader helped prepare me for the associate director position. The last time I did 4-H was when I was a kid growing up. We had some problems that had emerged in the 4-H program in Kansas and the dean at that time said, "Daryl, we need someone to open a conversation." That goes back to the trust.

He said, "We need you to open a conversation with our Extension agents across the state and try and see if we can't get the 4-H program moving forward again." He asked me if I would be willing to do that and just said point-blank to me, "Daryl, there's more trust in you amongst Extension agents." The agricultural agents were probably the group that was the most concerned about the 4-H program. He said, "Would you take that on?" I said, "Sure." Can't turn down a dean. I walked into that, and not having any background in youth development, not having any strong background in community development, that was one of the greatest learning experiences I have ever had on the job.

With all of the issues that you have with the events and activities and project areas and everything else that goes on in 4-H, there is always strife. I thought, "What do you use as the way to ground yourself so that you can operate with some stability in your decision-making processes?" I learned about the critical elements for positive youth development and that became my foundation.

If you would ask me a question about how we should handle this project or how we handle this controversial issue, I would pull that little card out that had all the critical elements of youth development and I would go down through those. Thinking through that and ask, "How might we solve this in light of our attempt to create a positive youth development experience? How best do we do that?" I found that that works for most decisions if you have that kind of a foundation. It caused me to look at community development differently because it is that trust element, and understanding what it is, that we are trying to accomplish. What are some of those foundational principles? How do you create the open dialogue and discourse? All those kinds of things were really necessary.

At that point in time, the associate director position came open. I felt like I was ready to take on the responsibilities of the entire Extension program and not just limit myself to our agricultural, ag and natural resources components of the program. I started in August 2004 and quickly realized that you do not know what it is to be in administration until you are sitting in that chair. It was probably somewhat less traumatic because of the experience of doing the 4-H prior to starting as associate director.

For example, when I walked into the first faculty meeting with all of the 4-H faculty and sat down with that group after I had agreed to carry on this conversation, there was enough tension and concern within that group that one of those faculty members said, "Daryl, are you with us, or are you just here?" I sat there quietly and I said, "I'm with you. The fact that I'm here, I'm with you. Now I don't know what you mean by 'with you' yet, at this point in time, but you can tell me more and I can help put a little more meat on that answer." I will tell you, that was a scary situation. That was after the dean asked me to help open up a conversation and when I walked into it I found out that it was a whole lot more than just a conversation that was really necessary.

The thing that taught me was that you have to have some sort of grounding to do these jobs in administration. You have to have something that is providing a rudder. That was the first time I had ever been in a situation where I knew I was outside my realm of subject-matter expertise in knowing and understanding how to solve problems. I floundered for a little bit, trying to find rudders, and then I found those rudders. That gave me that experience. I knew that was going to happen again as I stepped into an associate director role, so one of the first things I needed to do is to begin to find those rudders.

For anybody who is going into becoming a director of Extension, here is an experience that might help you immensely. When I started, we immediately went into a strategic planning process. We invited constituents, our nonemployee base as well as a cross-section of our employee base to come together to talk about how we sustain, improve, and build our Extension system for the future. I gave them a broad context and went through about three months with that group, designing and developing a strategic plan for the system.

From that, I have established what my priorities are. I also have that thing to fall back on—that document, that body of work to fall back on—to say, as I am making my decisions, "Are these going to help us to achieve those goals that were set out within that strategic plan, or not?" So it gave me a great set of guidance on where my priorities really ought to be set.

As an associate director, it did not take me long before I basically laid out three broad goals that I said the system has got to work on. Those three broad goals were: first, we have to improve the professionalism of the organization: shore up our professional development, shore up our training, and do all of those kinds of things. Second, we have to reengage in such a way that we create stronger local programs, whether that is through communications technologies, teamwork, or all sorts of other things to increase the capacity of our local Extension agents to be more engaged in stronger programming. The third was that we have to diversify—to become a friendly organization to people who do not look like us and go through whatever transformations are necessary.

Those three points seem to reverberate throughout the strategic plan. They were not necessarily the goals that were stated, but you could read them throughout. I pulled those out and said that is what I am going to be working on for the next several years. And they continue to be the things that I work on.

How did I learn that? I had the good fortune of being on a provost search committee before I ever got into this position. We had had an excellent provost at Kansas State University. He was stepping down; he was basically retiring from administration and going back to the faculty. When we were on that search committee, one of the first things we did was look at each other and ask, "What does a provost do?" We invited the current provost to come back to the table, and at that session, he talked about how you needed to focus your attention on your two or three or four priority areas. He said there is a host of other things that go on in this university, but in terms of where you are going to expend your time and energy, you have to have a set of priorities. When ideas emerge from the faculty that you can see you are going to support, you get in there and work with them. When they are working on other stuff, you just try and support however you can. But that is not your priority. Anyway, through that discussion I said, "Now he had not only described it, but he had practiced it." The faculty had a great deal of trust and appreciation for him as a provost. So that, too, was one of those guiding discussions.

When I started the strategic planning process, we had just gone through tough budgetary times—right at that 2000-2002 timeframe. There was some insecurity in all of that instability. That was the reason why, from a broad standpoint, it was about sustainability improvement. How are we going to need to look 20 years down the road to know that we will still have a strong, vibrant cooperative Extension system? What do we need to be looking for in the way of changing the organization? It came at a good time in that regard. We were not comfortable; there was a little angst. What came out of that process was working with new audiences and becoming a friendly organization to people who do not look like us—that's the way I put it.

The provost and I were engaged in creating a new center. Our dean and director who came on board about the same time I did was Fred Cholick. He had previously been the dean at South Dakota State University. I did not know Fred other than professionally: he is also in agronomy as his basic background area. Fred came on as dean and director, and Fred and I would have road trips together and we would start exploring that strategic plan and thinking about what all do we need to do.

Creating the Center for Engagement and Community Development

I kept talking about how we needed to figure out some way to strengthen our community development element. I said one of the things that Extension in Kansas needs some revitalization on is to put our Extension agents into more of a role as a community leader. It's helpful just being able to have your radar screen out, and know what is being discussed on Main Street, or what is being discussed across the county as the broader issues. Then you try to figure out how Extension supports the work in trying to solve those critical issues.

We got to talking about it from the standpoint that we knew there were other entities across this campus that could contribute to that. But one of the challenges was that, historically at least, they looked at us and said, "Well, Cooperative Extension is over there, and here's the rest of the campus." They would almost try to work behind our backs and in spite of us. In my previous work here I tried to knock down some of those barriers when I would get on campus committees and that sort of thing and would comment, and faculty would say, "You don't sound like somebody from

Extension." I said, "Why?" They said, "Well, you sound like you want to cooperate with us." I said, "I think I want to cooperate with you. I don't understand where you're coming from."

Well, the history had been that Cooperative Extension was its own entity. The rest of the campus had to do its various forms of engagement in spite of them. There was this idea of let's bring this together. As Fred and I talked about it, we said we really ought to bring everyone together.

We had one other model. We had created a center for ag resources and environment a few years earlier. We had done that within the ag experiment station and Extension. The individual directing that had seen ways to engage faculty from the broader campus, but it would take him a long time. I said, "You know, this is a conversation we really need to have with the new provost," because you could tell much of his philosophy was one of being a true land-grant. We needed to have faculty engagement.

I then went back into the strategic plan. There was one statement in it that said one of our goals would be that every faculty member across the Kansas State University campus would think of themselves as having an Extension appointment. I said, "If we're going to fulfill that, we're going to need help." We went to the provost, and actually it was an easy conversation. The toughest part was to figure out where we were going to put resources together. We were both in tight times from an economic perspective. But I think that, in those conversations, we both had full trust in each other.

We put resources together and created the Center for Engagement and Community Development. It actually operates out of the provost's office. That was the other thing that we said had to happen; it could not operate out of Cooperative Extension or it might be viewed as a college-of-ag thing. We needed it operating out of the provost's office, but in full cooperation, communication, and liaison with Extension. We took one of our community development faculty and adjusted that individual's appointment to where half of his time was to be spent with the center as engagement and community development director. This person was to operate as an assistant director to that center.

We put out a call for a national search, and one Saturday afternoon we were kicking off an Extension Walk Kansas Program in Manhattan, walking the circle at City Park. I happened to be walking it with David Procter. I had gotten to know David fairly well through various community development activities, and I knew he was really interested in all of this effort. He was asking me, "What kind of person do you think we need?" I said, "You'd be an ideal candidate."

He has told me since, that going back from that discussion and look-ing at it, and looking at himself in the mirror, he said, "You know this is something I could make a difference about." He became an applicant and he rose to the top with the search committee and the whole search process, and has been tremendous in fulfilling what I would say the agreed vision was. And that is that, while it is a "center" for engagement, it is more of a *catalyst* for engagement on this campus.

It is not a big office; it is not going to increase in size by itself. Instead, it is one of being able to look for all of the various opportunities, knowing what some of those needs are out in the state, having a sense of where faculty interests are, and trying to bring those interests together to work on various projects. The connection with Extension is just to say that when you get out there, there are Extension agents. You may not know them. They don't know you. We can help you develop that trusted relationship, and hopefully make your projects far more impactful than if you were just out there doing it yourself. And we've got lots of those kinds of examples.

Reflections on the Land-Grant Mission and Extension's Purposes and Work

All this links up with the land-grant mission. The phrase the *land-grant mission* is significant to me. It has a very positive, resounding element to it here at Kansas State University. I won't say I'm by myself in that. People talk a lot about the land-grant mission, who I would argue in many cases have totally different definitions of what it really is. But they speak of it in a very positive kind of way.

From my perspective, the land-grant mission really says that the out-comes of new knowledge, development, and the right kinds of learning environments have applicability to the people. And it is our responsibility as a land-grant university to see to it that the people have that opportunity, regardless of their economic well-being, regardless of whether they're a paying student. We have an obligation as a public, land-grant university to take that new knowledge and help the society apply it for public good. That to me is the uniqueness of a land-grant. It's seeing the obligation of taking new knowledge, new discoveries, and helping to translate that into something that has meaning for society. The land-grant mission is an obligation.

Other people have different views, because they'll compartmentalize it to say that it means you've got to take ag and home economics to the people. And that is not a comprehensive perspective of the land-grant mission at all.

The other part is I see it as a responsibility. And I've described it as an obligation to society. Our first obligation is to the people of the state of Kansas. Our next obligation is more regional, national, and global. There are some who would say that we just need to take it into the Manhattan community and test our theories and do our work. But one of the things that Dave Procter and I have talked about is that real engagement happens more than 50 miles from home, because you don't have that automatic trusted relationship in those settings. You've got to build that. And that to me says that there is an opportunity for it to spread more widely, because you've created that kind of relationship with a constituency that doesn't know you all that well as you walk in. And so we've got projects going in Kansas City. We've got projects going in Garden City. We've got projects going in various communities around the state, with various people from all walks of life.

Our rural grocery store initiative is a great example of the need to develop that trusted relationship with rural grocers from all across the state. At this stage I would say that, having done that, Kansas State University and the Center for Engagement and Community Development now has a trusted relationship with rural grocers all across the country. It's displayed in a way they know and understand the challenges we have in trying to maintain rural grocery stores. There are no easy answers. There may be thousands of answers, and they're helping us uncover them, helping us learn together, all those kinds of things. That to me is a great example of a true land-grant—we understand your problem, we'll work with you to discover the answers.

The land-grant mission has a lot to do with democracy, because democracy is all about free and open public discourse—public good, public interest. And I think in that regard we operate very much on a parallel with democracy. We have an Institute for Civic Discourse and Democracy at Kansas State. And I'm not at all ashamed to say that creating that institute is something Cooperative Extension should have figured out. But it came from another part of the campus, from David Procter and his colleagues. And it was already initiated when he was still a department head in arts and sciences. When I came to know and understand what that was all about, I said, "Wow, that's tremendous." A powerful model. It's a model that we use in Extension with our audiences. And we can certainly learn from that institute.

One of our Extension agents and I were talking earlier after an event with the Institute for Civic Discourse and Democracy. This is not a direct quote, but she said, "I thought that was just what we were supposed to do day to day, and now I find out that there is actually a body of knowledge that helps you understand how to engage with people in that kind of democratic discussion and dialogue? And there are different techniques that you can use? I just thought we were supposed to learn that on our own!"

That expresses the value that I see in the relationship with the Center for Engagement and Community Development. It lifts up other parts of this university and helps me see those kinds of resources that are in various places across this campus that have been well enough hidden that we just did not recognize them. The center helps to lift them up, and in many cases has made tremendous connections with what we're about in Cooperative Extension.

When I first read the "It's Not About the Rice" story in the Cornell publication, *We Grow People*, I was sort of taken by it because it drives home the point that we are about engaging people in gaining knowledge, gaining understanding, and figuring out how that can change their lives. And oftentimes we take a piece of work to them—teaching them how to cook rice, for example—and they take it to the next level. Now should we have known that was going to happen? I suspect that was the hope. But it goes so much further than learning how to cook a nutritious meal. It takes on the next dimension of building family. And then when you come back to the Extension agent, the Extension agent has observed that kind of a situation emerge. It's become an expectation. If someone asks an Extension agent the question, "What do you do?" and they say, "I teach people how to cook rice," for most of us, that's not much. But if you said, "I teach them how to build a family. You do that first by helping them put a meal at the table, and bring the family around the table." It's powerful. And I could look back in my career and I could say the same things happen. Building leadership capacity.

There was a young lady who got involved in a community just outside of Topeka in Shawnee County. The young lady got involved in her community and wanted to improve the community. She found out about the Kansas PRIDE program. And so in working some with us and with the Department of Commerce they decided in their community that they would put a PRIDE program in place in that community. She got involved, and she got on the board for the PRIDE program. And then she became a leader of that board locally. She's currently the chair of the Shawnee County Commission. She's coming out of a little town of maybe 2,000 or so, and the state capital in Topeka is part of her county. Through those experiences, she has grown to appreciate what she can contribute. She's become not just a member of the commission, but the chair of that county commission. I've got family that lives in that community, and they said, "We knew she had a lot of abilities, but she had never expressed them in that way until that course of events happened."

So how important is the PRIDE program? I don't know. That's the tough part. And that's the wisdom part of this whole job—to understand what the unintended consequences are in so much of what it is that we fund and so much of what it is that we do. And those positive spin-offs that do occur, and to understand what that all means in terms of the budgetary decisions that you make, and your priorities, and what you're going to fund and what you're not going to fund.

There are a lot of other spin-off stories to that community becoming part of the PRIDE program. There have been a lot of positive things happening. But with that individual, it's just interesting to see how that whole experience gave her confidence and showed her that she did have a gift that she could give back to the community to do some tremendous things.

That's what Extension work is about. They ask us for all of these numbers, and it frustrates me to no end because in doing so they seem to discount the importance of the stories. And Extension work is both. I mean we can create numbers, but I think the numbers always sell us short. It's the stories.

Later this week, over at the University of Kansas, they'll be having an economic development conference. They put one on each year. They've invited all the recent university presidents to come in there and talk about that very point: the return on the state's investment through education. And that concerns me if they're unwilling to look at what it means. And in the case of the university, what does it mean to put a student through a learning experience of attaining a degree? What happens to that student and that investment? K through 12 education is kind of in the same ballgame.

How do I describe Extension's fundamental mission and purpose? We're about changing people. And that comes through the vehicles that we use of agriculture, families, communities, and youth. But it's really about giving people the kinds of tools, the kind of knowledge, the ability to make decisions that . . . well, in the broadest context, it's to improve the standard of living and the economic well-being of the people of the state. That's the way I would describe it.

Many people would think of us as being fundamentally about agriculture, and transferring technologies, and that sort of a thing. I would say we're all of that, and broader than that. Because we could put all of our information into libraries or various other forms. It's our responsibility to create transformational learning that really matters, to create those kinds of environments to help individuals make critical decisions that can improve the public good.

Interview conducted by Scott J. Peters

A Thread Throughout Extension

A Profile of Sue Williams
Chair (Ret.), Human Development and Family Science Department
Oklahoma State University

In this profile, Sue Williams traces the growth of a deliberative ethic throughout her personal and professional life. By boldly and strategically persevering in the "uphill process" of securing the adoption of deliberative work in (and well beyond) the Oklahoma State University Extension system, she helps us see what is possible even in professional cultures that are dominated by what she refers to as "the expert model." Reflecting back on her work and experience as a "change maker" rather than as an "information purveyor," she helps us see how concepts of public deliberation have been an important— if sometimes neglected—thread throughout Extension's history. More important, she shows us how these concepts can be and have been interwoven in transformative ways with the kinds of scientific knowledge and expertise that universities generate and share.

My name is Sue Williams and I am currently the head of the Human Development and Family Science Department. I'm completing my third year as the head of the department. I have been at Oklahoma State University for 33 years—a long time. If I had to describe my content area of work as a scholar, before becoming an administrator, it was community-leadership development and citizen engagement through public deliberation. That

147

work wasn't something I've always done through these 30 years. When I was hired by Oklahoma State University, I came from Iowa State where I had a resident faculty position teaching financial management and resource management. I thought that I would do teaching and research similar to what I was doing at Iowa State. Through a series of life events, I ended up not accepting the initial job that they offered me and stayed out of the job market for a couple of years, but I'll say more about that later.

An opportunity came to join the Oklahoma Cooperative Extension Service during the energy crisis. My responsibility was to create a residential energy-management program through the Cooperative Extension Service, working collaboratively with agricultural engineering and agricultural communications. There was no long-term promise for the job and part of my job responsibility was to garner enough external funding to pay half my salary at the end of the first nine months. I took that challenge on and worked with an interdisciplinary team for more than 10 years. We created a program called the Energy Event that focused on energy management across the state of Oklahoma, in the farm sector, the industrial sector, and the residential sector. When the emphasis on energy management started to wane, I started doing environmental education work.

All of my work has focused on policy because that was my interest. I did my PhD while I was working on the Energy Event program. My dissertation focused on cost-benefit analysis of educating the public for making residential energy-management decisions versus subsidies, such as paying utility bills. Public policy questions have always been very interesting to me.

As the demand for energy-management programming and environmental education started subsiding in Oklahoma, I was able to start transitioning into work that was more along the lines of family community policy work and leadership development, in which deliberative work fits well. I ask myself, "How do you help community leaders be servant leaders? And also, how do you help them understand the critical role they play in helping the citizenry make decisions on their own behalf?" My career has evolved in response to those questions. And I've been working in the area of family and community policy and leadership development for about 20 years of my 32-year career.

To give some context, here is a brief snapshot of Human Development and Family Science (HDFS), the department I lead. There are actually three departments and a school in the College of Human Environmental Sciences. The college has approximately 2,200 students. The Human Development Department and Family Science Department has between about 500 and 550 undergraduate students from 65 to 70 graduate students. When I was hired as department head, the dean's mandate was to address financial difficulties in the department and, most important, to help members of the department create a focus for the department that would bring the five diverse disciplines of the department to a common mission and vision.

There are 60 faculty and staff in the department, with 30 of the faculty being tenure-tracked. The department has some clinical faculty with master's degrees who focus on teaching. HDFS has a Center for Early Childhood Teaching and Learning, which is a four-classroom center that takes children from 12 months to prekindergarten. It is a state-of-the-art child development facility working with both typically developing children and children with intellectual and developmental disabilities. The center prepares a large cadre of early-childhood educators and does child development research. The center is a very important and large part of the department. The department also has a center that focuses on marriage and family therapy, the Center for Family Services. This center is part of the Marriage and Family Therapy program. Students and faculty, or rather students supervised by faculty, have a client base that they work with on relationship issues.

HDFS has a mission statement that I think is important. This mission was developed after intense and sometimes contentious deliberation. Members of the department diligently worked on, and struggled, to develop and clarify our mission statement, and they developed a strategic plan based on the mission. Deliberative processes were used throughout the work to refine and focus the emphases of the department and to guide planning. The mission statement is: *Human Development and Family Sciences at Oklahoma State University will lead the field in applied interdisciplinary scholarship that reduces risk and enhances resilience among individuals and families across cultures and generations.* I know that's a mouthful, but it says a lot about the dedicated work of the department in five disciplinary areas.

Regarding the work of members of the department, there's a difference between a job description and how people describe their work—what they're really passionate about and committed to. I think it is pretty simple. I believe that most people hold the answers to challenging questions—and, frankly, their destinies—within themselves. Regardless of my formal title—faculty member, department head, mediator, or facilitator of deliberative work—my role is to help guide people to come to their own decisions based on what they already know. They just may not recognize that the answer to challenging questions is within each individual and the group of concerned people. The work of a leader is helping with that self-taught piece if it's at the individual level. Or if it's at the group level, then it's talking with one another to solve common problems. I don't see myself as a decision maker for others. I see myself as a facilitator, helping people talk through and work through issues to make things better for themselves or for the organization. This is the approach I took to meet the dean's mandate.

Getting to the role of faculty member and administrator at Oklahoma State is based on my previous experiences. I grew up on a large cattle ranch in western New Mexico. Actually, I grew up on three large cattle ranches. Each of these ranches were many miles apart. Employees did not manage the ranches. We had occasional employees, but our family managed the ranches. Our family had a unique situation in that during the school year, my brother, sister, and I lived on one ranch with our grandmother who was ill. This ranch was closest to town about 15 miles. My parents, during the week, lived on another ranch that was more distant or isolated. As children, we had the responsibility of the day-to-day activities of the ranch.

That kind of life was stressful, but it was also exciting. Sometimes it required conflict management. I was the oldest child: my sister is five years younger and my brother is six and a half years younger than I am. So I was the one taking the leadership role when we were alone as children.

Later we moved with our parents to another ranch 20 miles from town. I was about 12 or 13 years old when I started driving my sister and brother to town for school, because at least eight children needed to be on a bus route to justify the school system providing a bus. There were only three of us, so either our parents had to drive us to school, or my parents needed to negotiate an arrangement with local authorities to allow me to drive. Fortunately, there was only about a mile of state highway on the way to school so I was allowed to drive to town. The local sheriff and the state policeman knew what was going on, illegal as it was. The car was to go to school and never leave the school during the day. The only places the car could be seen were the grocery store, the post office, or the feed store. These trips always had to be made as we were leaving town to go back to the ranch. So at an early age, I started driving my siblings to school and we all assumed many responsibilities on the ranch.

There were many formative experiences growing up that help explain why I ended up getting interested in my current work. I think that the experience of driving to and from town helped me develop a sense of independence and of self-sufficiency. It helped me learn to analyze situations, to make stressful decisions, to make decisions relatively quickly, and to take responsibility for my decisions. I also learned that rules can be "bent." And along with that comes a grave responsibility to be a responsible person, because lack of responsibility on my part could have resulted in fatal results. I think having responsibility for my siblings' welfare, and for equipment and livestock helped me realize the complexity of decision making and the importance of input from others.

Many wonderful people influenced my development. Two particular individuals come to mind when thinking about deliberative work, one in a very positive way and one in a negative way. My paternal grandmother lived at the ranch that was closest to town. She was an extremely negative and vindictive individual. I learned some things about fairness, equity, and justice. Interacting with my paternal grandmother, who approached decision making from a dictatorial and matriarchal orientation, encouraged me to seek other more productive ways of making decisions. Her approach was distasteful to me, even at a young age. This negative experience has been a valuable gift to me, even though I don't think she intended to give that "gift."

The other person was an individual I interacted with when I was in the fourth grade. She had a child with a learning disability. During my early years of formal education, I attended rural schools that probably lacked quality. Thus, I didn't learn to read. I was labeled "a child with a learning disability." After working with me for a short time, Mrs. Martin said, "This child doesn't have a learning disability. She has not learned to read!" Mrs. Martin held my parents accountable and said, "You will provide a tutor. You will pack her lunch every day. I will work with her for half an hour during the lunch hour each day." By the time I reached the fifth grade, I was reading at a seventh-grade reading level. If Mrs. Martin hadn't come into my life and correctly identified the problem, I would have likely been a school dropout. We talk in public deliberation about identifying the problem. Well, my problem was not that I had a learning disability. My problem was that I couldn't read. After I got my PhD, I went back, I found Mrs. Martin, and I thanked her. And she said, "Oh, I didn't do anything." I often reflect on where I would be today if my life hadn't intersected with Mrs. Martin.

In deliberative work we analyze a situation and identify what the problem behind the problem is. The obvious problem was that I was not thriving in school. The problem behind the problem was that I couldn't read. We could also talk about quality of the school system and checks and balances, but I'll leave that discussion for another day. Fortunately, a wonderful educator was able to analyze what the real problem was with my individual situation and to correct it fairly quickly.

Based on the early experiences I have shared, you might not be surprised to know that I am a first-generation college graduate, and the only college graduate in my immediate family. Frankly, higher education was not highly valued in my family. Getting a high school education was important, but beyond that, not a lot of value was placed on higher education.

Fortunately, during my junior year in high school, I met a young woman on a Future Homemakers of America (FHA) trip. Her sister was in college, and she was college bound. I knew I was college bound, but I didn't know how I was going to get there. Fortunately, the young woman's older sister was very instrumental in guiding both Jayne and me toward college and helping us know what we needed to do, such as taking the ACT test and applying for scholarships. Jayne and I selected the same major and decided to room together. In the end, I think I would have made it to college, but meeting this young woman my junior year in high school helped me because she could give me specific guidance—guidance I did not receive from home or my public school.

After high school, I got my undergraduate degree at New Mexico State University. The first year of college was challenging and provided a culture shock. I came from a big rambling ranch house in the middle of nowhere, with lots of freedom and responsibility. Suddenly I found myself in a little tiny dorm room with many restrictions. Remember, I was the one who drove illegally at a young age. In college, I had a curfew. I wasn't particularly a night owl or a partier but it was fascinating to me that I had the level of independence I did when I was growing up, and the level of responsibility. And then suddenly I got to college and I had very little independence within a structured living environment. Just the reduction in the amount of space was a new idea, and being highly accountable for my comings and goings as a resident of a dormitory was foreign to me. I found this situation a little frustrating and of course found ways around the rules.

Aside from constraints in the living conditions, I liked the academic environment. Initially I was frightened because I came from a small, rural high school and was afraid that I would flunk out of college. The first semester I made the president's honor roll, because I was so afraid! From that time on, I enjoyed college life. Until I met my husband, whom I married my junior year in college, I maintained passing grades and not much more. After I got married that changed significantly. In three semesters of extremely heavy coursework, I went back up to a grade point that would get me into the master's program at Iowa State University. I was a Home

Economics Education undergraduate major. This was an excellent major in that it taught a variety of life skills topic areas. The major provided some ideas about what I wanted to do when I went on for advanced education. It also provided outstanding teaching methods. I think the knowledge and skills obtained at the undergraduate level have served me very well throughout my professional career. So I'm very proud of my Home Economics Education undergraduate degree!

How did I end up deciding I was going to go to graduate school? Well, I married my husband, whose name is Joe. He was finishing his master's degree at the time we met. I quit school with no intention of ever finishing my undergraduate degree. That was during the Vietnam War, and Joe was shipped to Germany to lead a Nike Hercules missile site attached to the Royal Netherlands Air Force. I was so excited to be going to Europe. I had hardly been across the New Mexico border, and suddenly, I was going to live in Europe. We lived in a very isolated kind of back-to-home community in northern Germany. We had to learn the ways of the community because we were not affiliated with any kind of a base. And so that was a really neat experience.

When we came back to the States after two years in Europe, I realized that I did not have a college education. I had the equivalent of a high-school education, and I wasn't going to go anywhere unless I went ahead and finished my education. So I went back to school at New Mexico State and made very good grades, allowing me to enter graduate school and obtain an assistantship. Joe obtained a research associate position at New Mexico State University, allowing me to finish my degree. During that time, I had a particular teacher who was important in my professional development. She was a young professor from El Paso, Texas, who taught personal financial management and resource management. She had a young family, commuted daily, and was able to successfully juggle lots of different balls. She was open with her students about both her professional and personal life. I liked the content area she taught, but I also liked her style. She seemed to be a woman who was well grounded with the ability to balance her personal life and her professional life. She worked well with college students. She identified with students very well and provided very good counsel. Ultimately, I went on to graduate school at Iowa State in the area of resource management and personal finance.

Joe was determined to get a PhD, so we looked at several universities. We looked at Purdue, Michigan State, Iowa State, and other universities. He was first accepted at Iowa State University. We were both able to obtain assistantships to finance living and college-related expenses. During our four years in Iowa we lived on a farm, learning about midwestern agriculture and the lifestyles of wonderful people.

Iowa was a very different experience from New Mexico. For the first time I was really challenged intellectually. Suddenly, I went from classes at New Mexico State where, if you applied yourself, you did very well because of the bell curve of student grades, to Iowa State, where I was attending classes with the cream of the crop from undergraduate colleges all over the nation. For the first time, I realized what true collegial competition was like. In my first statistics class I had no idea how hard it was going to be to compete with people who had come out of outstanding undergraduate programs. These graduate students held 3.95 or 4.0 undergraduate grade-point averages. For the first time in my life, I really experienced high levels of academic rigor and competition for grades. I kind of liked that—the environment frightened me but I liked it.

After Iowa we had opportunities to go to four different institutions. We had opportunities to stay at Iowa State as well as opportunities to go back to New Mexico State. We also had job offers at Texas A&M and Oklahoma State University. To help with a challenging decision we put together a spreadsheet highlighting opportunities and consequences for each choice. We decided that going directly back to NMSU probably wasn't a good idea. We also decided that staying at Iowa State, although we liked it there very much, was not a good idea because once a graduate student, always a graduate student. So we decided we needed to leave Iowa. Texas A&M, at the time was the highest-paying offer. But they actually had fewer opportunities for me. So we decided not to go to Texas A&M. We chose Oklahoma State kind of almost by default. We actually fell in love with Stillwater and with Oklahoma State University. We moved to Oklahoma in 1975 and never left.

I had my master's degree and had been teaching at Iowa State for two years while Joe finished his PhD. Iowa State had a policy of not hiring their graduates. Fortunately, the department had several retirements the year I graduated. I had been teaching as a graduate teaching assistant and had good teaching reviews. The department hired several associate and full professors to replace the retirees, and were short on funds to cover several classes. A fellow graduate and I were hired to split an appointment and teach large numbers of classes for something like $7,000 a year at Iowa State. That was a bargain for ISU, and a lot of money for me after living on a graduate assistantship.

When we went to OSU, I had a strong teaching and student-advising portfolio. I was offered a teaching position at OSU two days after I found out I was pregnant with our second child. We had a four-month-old, were expecting Number Two, my husband was taking on a new job, and we were moving to a new community. After careful consideration, I chose to decline that position. This was an extremely difficult decision for both Joe and me. I stayed home with our girls for two years. Then I had the opportunity to take a position with the Cooperative Extension Service, focusing on residential energy management. The position was a visiting assistant professor with responsibility for creating a new program area and bringing in enough external funding to pay half my salary.

In 1977, a position requiring fund development was unusual for my discipline. I decided to give this opportunity a try, and my colleagues and I were successful in procuring funding to support our programming and a portion of my salary. So my position and the work went on. We did contract work with the US Department of Energy and the Oklahoma Department of Energy. The energy management work started subsiding after about 12 years, probably in the latter part of the 1980s when I started doing some environmental education. I was always interested in policy and policy creation to address various challenging issues, rather than the nuts and bolts of how much energy a microwave consumed. From my perspective, the more interesting question was, "Is it better to educate people to manage their own energy resources or to pay their utility bills?" Addressing similar questions evolved into the work that I've done for about the last 20 years.

Why was I interested in the policy questions? I don't know. I think part of it was my training at Iowa State analyzing resource management from a household perspective within the context of the larger environment. How is a household impacted by decisions made at community, state, region, national, and international levels? Further how do household decisions impact the greater environment? As a society we are impacted not only by what's going on within that family unit, but what's going on far beyond the family unit.

The holistic education that I got at Iowa State stimulated my interest in looking at what factors within the family are impacting their well-being, and what factors outside the family are impacting their well-being and their decision making. In turn, how does the aggregate of micro-decisions impact communities and even the world? I think my preparation at the master's level probably set the stage for my interest in deliberative democracy.

When I joined Oklahoma State in 1977, a PhD was not required for a faculty member. Because I was an instructor at Iowa State, I was hired as an assistant professor with a master's degree. That would be totally unheard of today. It didn't take me very long to realize that if I was going to have a future at any kind of institution of higher education, I would need a PhD. It looked like higher education was where we were going to be, with Joe's interest in agricultural economics and his position. So if I was going to stay around higher education, I'd better get started on a PhD.

In 1979, I started my PhD in Environmental Science at Oklahoma State University. I was a full-time Extension Specialist managing a $250,000 external grant, had a child who was three-and-a-half and another child two-and-a-half, a fully employed husband, and decided to take on a PhD. But I did my graduate work slowly. It took me five years to finish my PhD. I got an interdisciplinary degree that was housed in the graduate college. My major professor was a welfare economist, and I was looking at issues related to the well-being of individuals in a broader environmental context.

Organizing the Oklahoma Partnership for Public Deliberation

Shifting then from my background to my more recent work with deliberation, Renee Daugherty and I have collaborated on doing deliberative forums and deliberative work over a number of years. Back when I first started with Extension, given that I had a background that was more finance and resource management, I did a lot of energy management work. Occasionally I was pulled in to help with other projects. In the late 1970s and early 1980s, Oklahoma was at the height of the farm crisis. Because of my background in finance and resource management, I was asked to help with work being done in agricultural economics addressing the farm crisis, particularly in the area of household finance. My colleagues and I were struggling because there was lots of blaming and frustration accompanied by an attitude that Extension needed to advocate for the farm sector. I was challenged to determine the appropriate role of a professional employed by a land-grant institution when addressing a difficult and emotionally charged issue. My colleagues and I were supposed to provide a balanced educational message that would provide a way of helping people working through the problem. I could provide factual financial information. Frankly, I had no clue how to address the emotional aspects of the issue. My rural, agricultural background complicated this dilemma.

In 1987, the Kettering Foundation produced an issue book on the farm crisis. I am not sure how I obtained a copy—destiny, blessing, or whatever. The issue book impressed me with the balanced way that this difficult issue was laid out. It had a balanced way of identifying the problem, the problem behind the problem, and then looking at alternative ways of addressing the problem from a variety of perspectives. At the time, I thought, "Man, this makes a lot of sense!"

I used the materials to frame presentations and news releases. I didn't understand much about Kettering or public deliberation. The materials were my lifeline for providing a perspective on the farm crisis that didn't focus on a side or on blaming. Even though I came from deep agricultural roots, it seemed to me the predicament that the farm/ranch sector was in was not a situation that one entity should or could be blamed for. There was responsibility from many sectors, and solutions would come from collaboration across sectors. It made sense to me that a multiple, balanced perspective was appropriate at an institution like Oklahoma State University. I still have that poor old book, and it is mighty dog-eared because I used it in lots of different ways.

I was very interested in learning more about the Kettering Foundation. I learned about the public policy institutes (PPIs). Given my job, the PhD, and my family situation, I couldn't take time to go to one of the institutes. At that time, there were about four to six being offered around the United States. I think there was one in California, but I'm not sure exactly where they were being offered. I'd look at those and say, "Well, you know, I really can't take time out to do that." So I didn't attend an institute while I continued to learn more about the broader framework for public deliberation. I started getting my hands on more issue books and used those. Later on there was one on energy that was really helpful to me. I actually used that one extensively, and conducted modified forums as educational events designed to help people understand the multiple perspectives surrounding the energy issue.

In the early to mid 1990s, the University of Oklahoma (OU) offered a public policy institute. I thought, bingo! This is right in my back yard. That is when I met Bob Swisher, Taylor Willingham, and Bob McKenzie. I met many of the "big players" who were foundational in deliberative democracy, and I was very impressed by the people and the concepts. Fortunately, Bob called me the next summer and invited me back as a faculty member. I felt honored to be invited back to learn more and share a little. I hadn't attended a workshop in Dayton and felt inadequate as a faculty member. Talk about flying by the seat of my pants! As a faculty member for the second OUPPI, I absolutely sweated bullets because I did not have the grounding that I think I needed to be a good instructor. I did learn from my colleagues as well as the participants, and based on my earlier work, did have something to share.

I taught at the OUPPI for two or three more summers. Sometime during that process, I attended one of the public policy institutes in Dayton and learned a lot more. Bob McKenzie was so helpful. I went to the session for people who taught for public policy institutes. I think the workshop was called the Directors' Workshop. Bob helped me dig down and understand the foundational pieces for some of the things I'd been teaching at a superficial level. I thoroughly enjoyed that educational and enlightening experience. Bob invited me back to teach during those sessions. Slowly but surely, from probably the mid 1990s on, I started developing the foundational work that I probably should have had long before I started actually doing deliberative work in the community. At this point, I had not facilitated a forum or organized a forum, other than the practice forums conducted during public policy institutes. I don't even remember the first community-based forum that I was involved in organizing or facilitating. It was sometime after I had spent a couple of years going to, and teaching, public policy institutes.

When I was using NIFI materials I was using them through my Extension work, particularly in leadership development. I was working a great deal with a group called Extension Homemakers (EH), a lifelong learning group. They were interested in hot topics, such as the energy crisis. The group wanted the content training. I found that using the issue books provided content and stimulated much deeper thinking about what people value related to the topic or issue. The NIFI framework on energy helped EH members think at a deeper level, often understanding the trade-offs and tensions related to the issue. At that time I did not conduct public forums with EH groups, but held discussions on the topic to stimulate deep thinking.

I first started moderating public forums in Oklahoma using the first issue book on energy. I believe it was called *The Energy Dilemma*. I remember being very impressed that people initially wanted the easy solution to challenging problems, and then changed their thinking as the forum progressed. As forum moderator, I helped forum participants develop greater depth of thinking about the issue. Moderators often talk about statements made by forum participants, such as "I've never thought about it that way" or "You know, it's somebody else's problem" or "If we only did X or Y, then the situation would be solved." Forum participation helps people understand the complexity and the depth of the problem, and how, as individuals, they own the problem. That whole evolution going in from "Well, if we would only do X, Y, and Z here in Oklahoma, then it would be fixed" to "Well, you know, it isn't that simple" certainly evolved out of that first public forum I conducted.

My work further developed in this area because OU decided to discontinue the public policy institute. This occurred somewhere around 1996. I had attended the public policy institutes in Dayton and had been doing work with Bob McKenzie. Bob called me and said, "We would like Oklahoma State University to take on the public policy institute." I was hesitant and think I frustrated Bob. As I observed the organization of the OUPPI—and I thought they did a very good job—it was all OU. I mean, other than some of the people invited in to help with the actual event there was no foundation that was broader than OU. And from my perspective, that is part of the reason it was discontinued.

I kept telling Bob that I wasn't really sure. He couldn't understand why, because Kettering was offering fiscal and human resources to get started. My reluctance wasn't because I didn't think this was a great opportunity for a land-grant university. I wanted it to be bigger than OSU. So I started talking to Renee Daugherty, because Renee and I are very good partners in that she looks at situations in a different way than I do. Her approach to decision making is different from mine. She's much more analytical and detailed than I am. I make decisions from a broad-based global view, while Renee focuses on details.

I talked with her about what I really liked about this opportunity and why I was concerned. After describing the opportunity, I asked her if she would like to join the effort. Fortunately, she agreed and joined conversations with Bob McKenzie. By then, we'd been talking for almost a year. I think Bob was ready to throw me out because I just wouldn't say, "Yes, we'll do it." Renee went to a public policy institute. She definitely resonated with the concept of public deliberation, based on what she and I had talked about. But then when she got there and learned more about it, she said, "This is definitely what a land-grant should be doing." So we decided to conduct what we called a capacity study with some funding from Kettering. We started designing the study in 1999, and we actually conducted the study in 2000. We started by identifying organizations and groups that seemed to have a mission that was consistent with principles of public deliberation. And then we got on the phone and talked to the leaders of those organizations. We described to them a little bit about what public deliberation was, how it fit the land-grant mission, and how deliberative work might help their organizations carry out their missions.

Over the course of several months, we talked with about 15 organizational leaders across the state of Oklahoma, including groups like rural electric cooperatives. The types of groups and organizations contacted were varied, covering educational and community service as well as state agencies. If we felt that there was a link between the concepts of public deliberation and what this organization was doing, we talked to the leadership of the group. If the leader of that organization concurred with our thinking, we asked them to identify 5 to 10 individuals within their organizations that were at the grassroots level of the organization. We wanted to get down to the "worker bees" and determine buy-in. Organizational leaders identified 5 to 10 individuals within their organizations who worked with citizens, not just state-level administrators or those in leadership roles.

Renee and I created a 13-question telephone questionnaire. We identified about 100 people representing 12 or 13 organizations. Then we worked with the OSU Bureau for Social Research to conduct telephone interviews to determine if local representatives saw the link between concepts of public deliberation and the work that they were doing directly with the citizenry. Furthermore, they were asked what kind of resources they would bring to the table. We weren't asking for money. We were asking such things as, "Would you be willing to help advertise a forum in your newsletter? Would you be willing to buy issue books? Would you be willing to provide public space for a forum? " We put this information on a grid representing all the resources offered by organizations and groups surveyed. We also considered all the people surveyed to determine if we had enough human capital and other nonhuman resources to sustain an Oklahoma Public Policy Institute. We concluded that there were enough individuals and groups across the state that resonated with concepts of public deliberation to create and sustain a PPI.

In May 2000, the first informational meeting was conducted with people who participated in the survey. Bob McKenzie, Ron Powers from Missouri, and others came to support the "two-day" briefing. This event was an overview of public deliberation, but it was basically a public policy institute for people representing potential partnering organizations.

In 2000, after the briefing, the Oklahoma Partnership for Public Deliberation was formed. It's still going today. It is a fluid organization with organizations and groups participating at various levels within a given timeframe. At any one time around 12 to 15 organizations are active in the OPPD. Some organizations, depending on financial situations or what they're doing, may ebb and flow in terms of their involvement in the OPPD. But it's still going and we still conduct forums, or rather that organization conducts forums across the state of Oklahoma.

When students were trained to make phone calls to invite individuals from various groups, they used a script highlighting concepts of public deliberation. The script focused on the idea of people solving their own problems and people coming together to discuss problems of common interest. Renee and I had already talked to these individuals and they agreed to participate in the 13-question phone interview. Organization representatives were asking if deliberation resonated with the work that they were doing at the local level.

When we were presenting this idea to people, it wasn't being presented as a Kettering Foundation project or an issue-book-centered activity. It wasn't issue-book centered at all. We did mention the Kettering Foundation but it was not like this is something that Kettering wants to do. The concept was born at the Kettering Foundation, but the idea of people coming together to discuss and address concerns of common interest went beyond the foundation.

Something else that is important is that this is what a land-grant should be doing. What I mean is that the whole idea of helping people address and solve problems by empowering people to solve their own problems is the mission of the land-grant. This is alongside extending the basic knowledge of the university to the citizenry while respecting their ability to make their own decisions. All of this was my understanding of what a land-grant was supposed to do. You provide people with basic information on any topic to inform them about the latest research-based information, but then beyond that, how might they use that basic information to apply it to their own situation, and ultimately come to a decision that they feel comfortable with and that fits their particular needs? This is at the individual level and extends to the community level as well.

One of the most interesting forums that we did many years later was called "Pathways to Prosperity." We used an issue book that wasn't even developed by Kettering. The Southern Growth Policy Board collaborated with Kettering on this framework. An OPPD Team went to Woodward, Oklahoma, which is in the western part of the state. That was when there was a decline in rural communities and there was a big push for economic development. Before the forum began, I stood at the door and asked every person who came—and there were about 40 people who attended that forum—a question, like "Well, are you for economic development?" Every person who came in the room said, "Yes, I certainly am an advocate of economic development."

When we started the forum, it was so amazing that there were 40 different definitions of economic development. There were 40 different thoughts about what people were willing to trade-off related to economic development. "Well, yeah, we want to develop this area, but we don't want to give up certain elements of our lifestyle." And those elements of lifestyle were different from person to person. This group of people, who all agreed initially that they were for economic development, had different personal definitions of economic development and what it looked like to them. For that group to come to common ground about what economic development would look like in Woodward, Oklahoma—what the citizenry could live with—would take work beyond the forum. After the forum, the ideas about economic development were different from any definition that a person brought in to that meeting. Instead, it was some combined thinking about what they could and could not live with. So it was kind of the evolution of a different definition—certainly not a definition of economic development that came from the university.

That's one of the stories that is so interesting to me. I think people at the university level had a certain definition of what economic development would look like. And every person who attended the forum had a definition of what they thought economic development would look like. During the course of the forum, that definition changed or was modified. The group came to more of a common understanding of what economic development would look like in Woodward, Oklahoma. This forum was held during the days of consignment animal operations, whether it was hogs or cattle. Many people thought, "Oh, well, if we only had a consignment hog operation, we could fix it." I mean, that was the simple solution to economic development needs. During the forum, participants were going, "Well, you know, it's a whole lot more than that. It's a whole lot more complicated than that." More important, we didn't organize that forum. It was probably one of the partners in the Oklahoma Partnership for Public Deliberation, a rural electric cooperative.

As I think about the other forums that I've been involved in, I recognize that they all have a character that's very unique. There were two questions that were before the Oklahoma legislature several years ago. One dealt with gambling (the lottery) and another with same-sex marriage. The Oklahoma Partnership hosted a series of forums to try to help broaden thinking on the issues. We used the gambling issue book produced by NIF for one set of forums. I think we used material from Public Voice for same-sex marriage. The framework was modified to reflect the Oklahoma situation. Forums were conducted on college campuses and in communities across the state. Mixed participation was welcomed and encouraged in either venue.

I think these forums had a big impact whether or not you agree with how the vote went. I think people who participated in the forums had a better understanding of the broader issues surrounding both gambling and same-sex marriage. We did not call the forums on same-sex marriage that. We chose a very different title than "Same-Sex Marriage." I think we called them "The Definition of Marriage." The OPPD wanted the issue to be broader than same-sex marriage. We worked very hard to try to provide something that was beyond a "yes or no, or I'm for it, I'm against it" discussion. Our objective was to broaden the thinking about that particular issue.

Another series of three forums was hosted by a group called "Stillwater Speaks" dealing with the alcohol issue. There was conflict or tension between the university and the community on the issue of alcohol, and particularly about what was going on in student-occupied housing off the Oklahoma State University campus. This series of forums used the NIF Alcohol framework with a data sheet specific to the Stillwater Community, including OSU. Invitations were sent to specific individuals and organizations in an effort to include a cross-section of the community in the deliberations. Forum participants included junior high, high school, and college students; community leaders; landlords; agency representatives; parents; city officials; and university officials.

Stillwater Speaks worked hard to involve a web of university and community stakeholders, similar to James Fishkin's methodology. Information gathered from forums regarding what people were willing to do and not do were used to guide a decision-making session involving university and community leaders focused on the community's roles and responsibility and the university's roles and responsibilities related to student alcohol use, on and off campus. I felt that the three forums helped inform the decision-making process in a positive way.

I believe that the moderator has a very important role in public deliberation. I also think the framework helps create a thorough, deep, and balanced conversation on a complex topic. It is important that people come to forums with a high level of care and passion about the issue so that it's a very real discussion relevant at individual and community levels. It's also important to create a space where diverse people can discuss the issue in a civil manner, and respectfully consider the different perspectives on that issue. A good example is the series of forums hosted by Stillwater Speaks on same-sex marriage. During the forum, parents of children who were professed gays and lesbians said, "You know, I never thought that I would ever be talking about this from the perspective that these are real human beings needing societal support."

A variety of elements help facilitate public deliberation. From my perspective, two are vitally important. First is the skill of the moderator in being able to respectfully accept comments that have a strong emotional flavor, putting them in a context that helps other members of the forum respect the passion and also hear the message that is connected to the comment. Second, I think the framework helps the moderator pull from perspectives that are within the framework, even if those perspectives are not coming out at the moment in the forum. Usually pointing out perspectives in the framework will elicit other perspectives from members of the forum, without the impression that the moderator is biased or presenting personal perspectives on the issue.

Reflections

When I reflect on how this work has been adopted by the Oklahoma Cooperative Extension System, I must say it has been an uphill process. Several county Extension educators in all program areas have used public deliberation to educate and address public controversy. People like Claude Bess, District Extension Director, and Leland McDaniel, a county Extension director, provided significant leadership in helping Extension educators understand, appreciate, and use public deliberation at the local level. Deliberative work occurred in pockets across the system until the water issue emerged a few years ago. Until that time, it had been difficult to help higher levels of administration in Extension understand the applicability of deliberative principles across all content areas of Extension and the land-grant institution.

Water has been an issue off and on in Oklahoma for many years. Extension was asked to assist in determining public perspectives for the development of a statewide long-range water plan. It was at that point that administration realized that water is an issue that is more complex than gallons used by various sectors. Understanding accessibility, ownership, and water rights meant that addressing the water issue using an expert-model was not going to work. That is when Renee, Claude, Leland, and I were approached. Leaders in Extension and several state agencies said, "We think this is the way we need to approach the water issue in Oklahoma." That statement demonstrated an important level of understanding of public deliberation on the part of Extension administrators, and other leaders across the state. The Oklahoma Partnership for Public Deliberation was established in 2000 and aggressively supported public deliberation. The question of using a deliberative model on the water issue came in 2005. Until then there had been little universal recognition by Extension of the potential for public deliberation for a hot statewide topic. Renee Daugherty took leadership for this project.

Many think Extension works from an expert model. Is that what's going on? Yes and no. If I understand why I was hired back in 1977, it was to help people use accurate information to make sound decisions on their own behalf. As my career in Extension evolved, I observed deliberative principles being used at varying levels. I also think that Extension professionals have applied the expert model because, frankly, it's easier. I do believe concepts of public deliberation, not called that, have historically been a thread throughout Extension. Deliberative concepts have been applied in various ways over time as Extension professions have worked with clientele to work through challenging problems.

Extension professionals who understand or appreciate the idea of people being the masters of their own destiny are the ones who resonate with concepts of public deliberation, and use them in their Extension work. These individuals understand and respect that the research base will help people make their own decisions. I don't think public deliberation and the expert model are contrary. Rather it is how expert information is used in the decision-making process. I do think there are enough people throughout Extension in Oklahoma that appreciate concepts of public deliberation. However, I don't think public deliberation permeates the system.

Extension is sometimes perceived as an organization that simply gives people fact sheets and information. I think most Extension professionals are committed to helping people figure out how information can be used in their particular context. From my perspective, that is part of our responsibility as facilitators or change makers. There was a book written many years ago about the role of the Extension professional, at the state level or the county level, as being a change maker. Well, there's a lot of difference between an information purveyor and a change maker.

So that makes me ask the question: what is the land-grant mission? What does it mean? I believe that the land-grant mission is to engage the citizenry and provide people with resources to help them make decisions that improve their well-being, whether it's in agribusiness or it's personal financial management. Our work is to provide people with the tools to make their lives better. People talk about the land-grant mission at Oklahoma State, but there are many different understandings. I think there's a lot of variation of understanding.

I'll give you a little bit of an example. I'm responsible for doing the appraisals of faculty and staff in this department. The departmental promotion and tenure document clearly states that each faculty member has a responsibility for all three elements of the OSU mission. I'm the first department head in the college with an Extension career before becoming an administrator. During the appraisal process I hold faculty members accountable for the substantive work that they are doing to fulfill their outreach/engagement responsibilities. This stance has mixed levels of support. Fortunately, upper administration in the college supports my perspective on the importance of outreach and engagement.

Some faculty members report, "My outreach was giving a 20-minute talk to a local civic group." From my perspective this is a very limited view of outreach and certainly does not constitute engagement with the community. On the other hand, an early career faculty member based in Tulsa talked with great passion about his work with the local Boys and Girls Clubs. His background is human development and he spoke about how he has used his expertise to "engage" (I use that word carefully) youth and their families that are in homeless shelters and also involved with Boys and Girls Clubs. This faculty member brings his knowledge and expertise to individuals and families in a way that they're able to find some tools to improve their situation. I laughingly said to him, "I give people credit for running out to the Rotary Club and doing their little spiel, because I think that may be a start. However, you understand the concept of a land-grant where you engage people and help them with your training to improve their situation." This faculty member is truly engaged with the community.

I made a difficult decision to transition to an administrative role and give up my Extension programmatic responsibility. Initially, I tried to maintain my Extension work along with my administrative duties. I had wonderful colleagues in Extension and the Oklahoma Partnership for Public Deliberation who assisted with my Extension appointment. In the end, I concluded that I could not do justice to both administration and Extension programming. As an administrator, 15 percent of my appointment is for overseeing the departmental Extension program. I've written a job description for a family and community policy position. Deliberative work is heavily embedded in that job description. And right now, I am lobbying Extension administrators very hard to fill that position. The economic situation across the United States. and in Oklahoma isn't good and funding has not been approved for the position. I believe the position will eventually be filled hopefully with a person grounded in public deliberative work.

Interview conducted by Scott J. Peters

Guides by the Side

A Profile of Jan Hartough
State Coordinator for Public Deliberation Chair (Ret.)
Michigan State University Extension Service

Throughout much of her career, Jan Hartough and her Michigan State University colleagues engaged in community development and public deliberation as "guides by the side." Through a story about her work with a community that was struggling with the divisive issue of deer management, in this profile Jan shows us what "guides by the side" and their nonacademic colleagues can accomplish by working together when things get tough. In her reflections on the story, she discusses why she stresses the importance of attending to the realities of specific, local situations in deliberative work instead of just implementing "models" and "best practices" developed elsewhere. There is wisdom in this lesson for professionals of many kinds who want to understand how they might, as David Mathews puts it, "do what they usually do a bit differently, so that their work reinforces democratic practices."

My name is Jan Hartough. I'm the state coordinator for public deliberation for Michigan State University Extension. I'm also still doing some community development work in Barry County. That's the county that I was Extension director in for 25 years.

I grew up in Danville, Illinois. That's the home of Dick Van Dyke and Chuckles candies and Flamingo hair pins. Those were made famous in

Danville, Illinois. I had a great bringing up. I will say that when I was in high school my father was very involved with politics and ran for public office. At a fairly young age I became pretty involved in the public policy arena as far as seeing it from the side of somebody running for public office at the county level. We would stuff envelopes and we would have to go to all the local fairs and things like that. We had signs on our car and all of that type of thing. Then later on when I was at the University of Illinois, my dad used to make me come home just to vote!

I guess I had exposure to that whole public arena. I was really fortunate. I met Senator Dirksen and some real statesmen back then. My parents, because they were so involved, were invited to the governor's mansion for special things. I never thought about it much back then, but I do think those experiences had an influence on some of the things I've done.

At the University of Illinois, I was going to be a dentist. Then I switched over. Actually, I have a bachelor of science degree. I took all the science courses, and then I switched over to a business major. The person that was influential in that decision was my 4-H leader. I was in a city 4-H group. My mother wanted to make sure my sister and I knew how to cook and sew. We had the coolest 4-H leader. She had a big influence on my life. Her name was Madeline Yeager. I don't even know if she's still alive. I don't think they even live in the area anymore. She thought I would be really good in that whole arena of nutrition. I did enjoy that. At the University of Illinois, I was in a sorority, Kappa Delta.

I graduated at a good time, when jobs were a little more plentiful. One of my professors at the University of Illinois recommended a couple of positions for me to apply for. I got interviews for those. They flew me to Ohio. I interviewed in Columbus, Ohio, for the Columbia Gas System. Then they flew me to Toledo where the job was and offered me that position as the home economist for the company. I had to decide if I really wanted this job because I didn't know anybody in Ohio. Long story short, I took that position.

My professional name was Betty Newton, because that was what they called their home economist. Being in a large metropolitan area, it was sort of like synonymous with Betty Crocker. You were like an instant celebrity when you were out in the community. People would go, "Oh, I thought Betty Newton was much older." Here I was right out of college.

That was a phenomenal experience because they put you through extensive training. I had to spend several weeks with higher ups at their Columbus office being trained. I had some phenomenal opportunities in Toledo. I did work with famous chefs like James Beard and Craig Claiborne. Both chefs were in for special presentations in Toledo that were sponsored by the Columbia Gas Co. I got to head that up and organize it and all of that kind of thing. That was pretty scary for a kid just out of college. Here I was put into some really heavy-duty community kinds of things. It was the company's name on the line if I screwed up. On the other hand, when you think about it, those were probably building blocks for things that I went on to do later on because it forced me into knowing how to handle big-time affairs.

I met my husband in Ohio. Then he took a position in Michigan. We moved to Michigan. I didn't have a job right at first. I then worked as a nutrition instructor for Kellogg Community College and sort of got my feet wet with networking. We were in Battle Creek, Michigan. That was a phenomenal area because of all the food companies. They had what was called "home economics" back then. It's "consumer sciences" now. Because Kellogg was there, Ralston was there, and Post was there—all of them are in Battle Creek—there was a professional organization for home economists. I was networking with people from the Kellogg Company. That's how I met the person who was in the home economics position with Michigan State University Extension that I would eventually get. She told me she was leaving her position because they were moving up north, and that I ought to apply. Long story short, I got that position. I was a regional home economist.

I was housed in Calhoun County, which is where Battle Creek is. My office was in Marshall, Michigan. I worked a four-county area. I also did work in three other counties, even though there was a professional in all of those. We did a lot of programming together. I was there for 10 years. I felt like I was doing two jobs because they started a new program, which at that time was called the Expanded Food and Nutrition Education Program. I ended up having that with three different offices and a staff of 12 or so, plus doing the more general family consumer science work in the county.

I was ready for a change, so I applied and got the director's position in Barry County. About that time, too, I went back and got my master's degree at Michigan State University. What was interesting about that is that I did it in a totally different arena from what I had been doing. My master's degree is in public policy and adult education. I even did work at the state capitol as part of my master's work.

I think what influenced that was the fact that Michigan State University was pretty unique back when I started with them in that they had an emphasis on public affairs and public policy education. I got some unbelievable training in that arena, not just a one-shot thing. These were two-year programs. After that, I developed a curriculum called, "We the People, Your Involvement in Local Government," that won a National Farm Foundation Award. Our national professional association was one of the first to win this award.

It was also around this time (the late 1980s) that I met Jon Kinghorn from the Kettering Foundation at a national Extension conference. After learning more about the deliberative process from Kettering, I became very involved. As a result, when I became the National Vice President for Public Affairs for the National Extension Association of Family Consumer Sciences (NEAFCS), I held some workshops to introduce NEAFCS to National Issues Forums (NIF). Later we worked to set up an NIF Institute at MSU. So the deliberative process has been important to me for a long time.

Gradually, I started as county Extension director being involved a lot more in the community and having to address some very critical issues. We had formed a futuring group in Barry County, which I think is kind of unique. I don't know too many counties that were doing that type of thing back then. Also we did a lot of work with water issues. Our rural county had a GIS system that was kind of phenomenal. Grand Rapids and Kalamazoo didn't even have stuff like that back then. We were really moving ahead.

I gradually got heavily involved with land use issues because we were surrounded by four metropolitan areas. It was like either our farmland and everything was going to be gobbled up, or else we were going to band together. I did a lot of work with public officials in bringing them together to talk about what needed to be done. We were successful in being able to do some multi-township ordinances for protection of rural parts of our county.

Then I got heavily involved with economic development. Through the university I was able to bring in an assessment team. As a result of that, we formed an economic development alliance. Our chamber went from just being a city chamber to a countywide chamber. There were some real major changes that were brought about.

Also, way back in 1989 we had a grant from the W. K. Kellogg Foundation to Extension in a nine-county area on the western side of the state. Barry County happened to be part of that. Basically, Kellogg had said that they did not see the leadership that was going to be needed in the future from the western side of the state. They knew that the growth area for Michigan would be on the west side. All of these predictions have come to fruition. In this nine-county area, we were given small grants. They didn't tell us what to do, but you could use them for intergovernmental work. You could use them for leadership development and also technology.

I wanted to develop a Leadership Program for Barry County. I formed a steering committee. You do all those things you're supposed to do, you know. It was just a good idea. The steering committee said, "Yeah, great idea, but you don't have enough money." That was great because I had one of our judges on the committee who was able to get me a matching grant. In 1990 we launched our Leadership Program. It's still going today. It's been the real glue for the community. We were just able to do a longitudinal survey and study. It's phenomenal. I just feel really, really proud of being able to help get all of that started. The community has totally bought into it now. It's really embedded in the community. I think it's rare to find a community where something like that happens.

Actually, after about three years or so, we suspended leadership for a few years, because of a request of the commissioners. They had asked the leadership and the futuring group to work together to form what we called our Barry Community Resource Network, which ended up being made up of all our human services, and to help them coordinate that. That's still in existence today.

After a few years, the community came back and said, "We've got to get the Leadership Program back online." Then we restarted it. It's been going ever since. What's really cool now is that I think you can probably go to anything—any committee meeting, any board meeting, if you're Rotary, Kiwanis, whatever—and you just ask people if anybody's been through the Leadership Program, and you'll always have people standing up. Now you're seeing a lot of those people really moving into key positions in the community. That's exactly what we hoped would happen. Usually you're not in an area long enough to see that happen. Being director for 25 years meant I was very privileged in that I was able to work with community people and see a lot of things come to fruition. You really feel like you've helped make a difference. It's not me making a difference; it's working with my fellow citizens making the difference.

There's a ton of things that have happened in Barry County. I think because the population of the community is now 59,000, and being surrounded by four metropolitan areas that each wanted a piece of Barry County, it was sort of like David and Goliath. We always kind of felt like, doggonit, we're going to do this even if they won't give us any money. Unfortunately, there were a couple of times that we didn't get some grants. Later, in talking to some of those people, they said, "Well, we knew that you guys were going to do it one way or the other anyway." It's sort of like in a way that wasn't fair, but they were absolutely right.

We were very fortunate, too, in Barry County in that a lot of people have been there for a while. Even outsiders that have come in got involved bringing new perspectives with them. They really got involved with community things. As things arose, it was like you just sort of knew who to bring together and to at least plan it, so that you could broaden it and bring in more of the public, especially when we were dealing with land use issues.

For almost two years we did a lot of educating. We went to township meetings. We did public meetings, just helping people understand what was happening with land use issues in Barry County and what might happen in the future. We did build-outs of our work with our planning and zoning person. We had very visual presentations. We once had a large seminar. We had something like 90 officials all in the same room. That had never happened before. As a result of that, we ended up with a citizens' group that formed that had 80 or 90 people who were concerned with land use issues.

I just have to tell you a little caveat here because in Extension we were so far out there in working with the community on raising awareness that when I reported to the commissioners, we had a couple of commissioners that really put me on the spot as far as what was going to happen next. We had action groups that formed. One of them was around land use. They were like, "What's going to happen with these action groups?" I said, "I don't have a clue. It will be up to the citizens in the groups that have formed. All we have done is the educational part, helping people understand what's going on in the community." They just kept needling me. It ended up being front page news. We were like, "Oh my gosh. What's going on now?" I had to back off a little bit from land use stuff.

What was cool is that the citizens just picked up right there and moved forward. They were really upset because we had three or four commissioners who weren't in favor of any of the land use regulations. In the next election five of them were voted out. The ones that got put back in office all were pro land use planning. That was very critical. It's been key for the county ever since to have commissioners who realize the need for land use planning. That was huge, really huge.

I was county Extension director for 25 years and very much a part of the Barry community and involved in a lot of things that went on there. I will also say, that part of my education was having international training. That was a two-year program through Extension. Again, it was a Kellogg grant that the university received. That made a profound change in my outlook on things. I went to the Netherlands to study land use issues and was able to bring that information back. When we did work in Belize I was able to get our local Rotary involved. For three years, we sponsored two schools in Belize and did things there.

I took a sabbatical because I wanted to do some more with leadership development work. During that time I became involved with Ireland. That's been a 10-year engagement and is still ongoing. I did community development work with them as guides by the side working in 12 very rural communities that knew that they weren't going to get anywhere unless they all came together. Collectively, they only represent 10,000 people. They form what's called the Tochar Valley Network and Rural Community Network. It's phenomenal what's happened there. Again, they have done the work. We've just been guides by the side. We have quite a few programs. Also through that I was able to introduce them to public deliberation. Now we have people coming from Ireland over to Kettering. That has been phenomenal. Then I worked with them to develop the issue of alcohol misuse. Now they're moving on to doing something with drugs. They got a grant. That's really taken off.

With the community development work over there, it's been phenomenal. We've done everything from value-added things dealing with their farmers, to figuring out other ways to bring income onto the farm, to creating trails and ecotourism. It just goes on and on. They've gotten into organics. That's been part of our work with them. They didn't know they were doing this, but they're actually doing CSAs (community-supported agriculture) right now. They said, "What's CSAs?" I go, "It's what you're doing."

Now I'm in the process of just working with them. I've been asking the probing questions. "Have you thought about . . .?" Because they're into organic foods, they hadn't even thought about perhaps providing cooking classes or classes in food preservation. Now it's pretty exciting. They're thinking of all of these ideas and expanding. The cooking part could be international, promoting the idea that people in the States could come to a rural community and be able to learn how to cook some Irish food as well as maybe go on one of the trails they've developed through the farmers' fields.

I'm just going into my third year of serving as the state coordinator for public deliberation in Michigan. I started in August of 2007. For almost a year prior to that we had been talking with Kettering, back and forth. Kettering was very interested in whether it's possible to embed public deliberation in an organization like Extension. Also, can you do more with public deliberation in a university setting in general?

We entered into a three-year research agreement. It's with our ag experiment station, Extension, the College of Ag and Natural Resources, Kettering, and the College of Arts and Letters. We dodged the bullet so we didn't get zeroed out. We were talking about that the last time we were down at Kettering. Extension now is going through tremendous restructuring as is as the College of Ag and Natural Resources. How that's all going to shake out we really don't know. A lot of that is going to be taking place after the first of the year.

I think the good thing is the fact that then my responsibility was to build the capacity within our Extension educators to do deliberative work in their communities dealing with controversial issues, especially in the ag and natural resources arena. I just had to hit the ground running and develop a training that we call "Addressing Community Issues." That's a two-day training. Then another one-day we do on issue framing, which is a quick framing.

Knowing my colleagues, I knew that they could not take a year to frame an issue. You don't have that kind of time if you're dealing with a controversial issue in your community. I really like the quick framing; you have something right away and your community can start the deliberation. You can start the conversation back and forth. I've been doing that.

Along with that, then, we're also doing some stuff with bovine TB. Then on the horizon on the cellulastic plan in the UP, they released a $2 million grant to Michigan State University and the Michigan Tech Institute. We're probably still going to be doing some deliberative work in that arena. It's been two years now, so we've laid a lot of the ground work. We have over 100 of my colleagues that we've been able to train so far. I just got a call from up in the Charlevoix area. They've got a really hot issue that's pretty controversial dealing with trails. Hopefully we'll be able to work with them a little bit up there. We're still doing some stuff that's heating up in the animal welfare arena. I'm not sure where that's going to go.

All of this stuff is bubbling along with trying to do the trainings and everything else. You'd think you'd have a little down time, but it's just been constant. Now I can't believe we're entering our third year. Things are really starting to pop. That's what happens. There's sort of an incubation period. Just because you do training doesn't mean that it takes right away, especially in this area of public deliberation. I think as long as it's in the back of people's minds, then as situations arise they're thinking, "Ah, I think we can apply this process here." That's what's exciting. We're starting to really see some of that now.

The Grand Haven Project

With that said, now I will focus on my work in Grand Haven. I think it was in January 2007 that the City of Grand Haven was having trouble with overpopulation of deer. Grand Haven is an upscale resort area. They had several deer in the downtown area that had actually gone through plate glass windows. People were like, "Something has got to be done!" People would have maybe 25 deer in their yard. All their hostas and plants were getting eaten up. There were people hot under the collar. Apparently the city had a public forum. It was awful. It was very polarized. People were yelling at each other. That's what happened. Then everybody went away thinking that the city commissioners were going to do something, and they really didn't do anything.

As time went on, people were still grousing. We were just entering into this public deliberation stuff. The ag agent there in Ottawa County had called Frank Fear and me, and asked if we'd be willing to maybe work with the group. We said, "Well, okay. We need to get more information." We set up a meeting. They had a party for me for my 25 years as the county Extension director, and the very next day I had to be in the Grand Haven meeting with the city of Grand Haven officials as well as the officials from the neighboring city of Ferrysburg. We had a discussion about what was going on. We outlined what we could do, and said that we did not have pat answers. They agreed to let us help.

In August 2007 we started meeting. From September through October we held three community forums. They were roughly two hours each. What we did at those is that we kind of did a "deer management 101." We had one of our urban deer management specialists from MSU do a visual presentation for the public. Then I facilitated the public forum. What we did was we just simply had blank newsprint everywhere across the stage to write down what we heard. We asked people, "What concerns you with the deer issue?" We just got all of that out. I asked them about what might be possible approaches. And we got all of that out.

Then the city appointed a task force. On the task force, there were several people who wanted all of the deer to be killed. There were several people who didn't want any deer to be killed. And there were a number who were neutral. Our first meeting with the task force, I brought all of the information that we had gathered from the three public forums. I put the task force into work groups going through all of that, identifying the common themes that were coming out. Basically, it came out to about five areas. Then we just kept meeting with them to solidify. If you think about it, we really started framing the issue. We got citizen input in September and early October. We had to do a preliminary report back to the city commission December 3. We were really moving fast in working with this group.

The concerns, that fall, were social perception, public health, eco-logical damage, and domestication of deer. As we worked with them the approaches ended up being public education, habitat modification, increased social tolerance, and deer herd management. In working with them, I used all the things you do in a framing. We were true to the information that came from the public. I said, "So what did the public say about education?" We listed all of that out. What might be some recommendations to the city commission? We asked things like, "Do we need some more information?" In all of these areas we did that. Then we said, "Okay, if you did some of this . . ." Like when they were talking about habitat modification, one of the recommendations was to have the city council revise their law from six-foot to eight-foot fences. Was that even feasible? We said, "So-and-so, you'll need to try to get this informa-tion." We were working with an assistant city manager. "Can you get us that information? Is that even possible?"

It was all of that back and forth thing: "Do we need more information?" Then I would say, "Well, okay, if you do this, what might be the conse-quences? Are there going to be any costs to this?" That's how we worked through this.

We were really doing quite well. We came up with preliminary recom-mendations. We had the task force report out to the city commission. The city commission was really pleased with the progress that was being made. They had asked for the final report March 2008, which still only gave us a couple of more months to work on it.

Things were progressing fine until right after the first of the year when one of the people on the task force who really felt more needed to be done in controlling the deer—in other words, shooting more deer or culling more deer—took it upon herself to write a letter to the editor. She didn't say any-thing to Frank and me. She didn't say anything to the rest of the task force. You can imagine the next task force meeting, people were hot. This is where emotions really start coming out. A real trust level had started to build with that group.

Prior to January and that first report getting out, we had the person who was feeding the deer say, "I understand now why I really shouldn't be feeding the deer." She was no longer feeding. We had the person who was definitely against culling saying, "Well, you know, after learning everything with this, I can understand that maybe some culling would have to be done." Those were huge moves within that group.

Then January comes, and people were very upset. They said to the woman who wrote the letter to the editor, "Why did you do that?" She said, "Well, it was my opinion. It wasn't the task force." They're going, "But people know you're on the task force. They're going to think that maybe some of that was the task force's view." She was trying to say no, it wasn't, and just sort of trying to deny it. When that happened, it caused the start of a split within the task force. The ones that really were against culling started banding together. So it became more polarized at that point. Talking with each other outside of meetings and things like that. If people wanted to come to those task force meetings, we had to allow them because of the open meetings law. We asked them to not sit at the table, because they weren't part of the task force. They could sit on the outer part. One of them, we found out, was a real rabble-rouser and didn't even live right in the Grand Haven community. She was a friend of one of the people on the task force. I didn't know this until afterwards, but she was passing this person on the task force notes, like what to say, or "Bring this up," or whatever.

When we came to the hardest issue, which was the culling (prior to that they had kind of agreed on five triggers for culling) they were trying to get it down to specifics. That's when I thought the whole thing was going to fall apart. We had this one meeting just on culling. They totally agreed on all the other stuff. Here we were with the culling. They decided they couldn't agree, because we had one person on the task force who said, "Well, it's going to have to be X number of deer per square mile before you cull." This person was not basing it on research. Normally the meetings were two hours. This night after three hours I finally called it. I said, "It's obvious you're not going to agree." They had shared their preliminary results with the public. Now they were going to change all this stuff in the culling. I said, "The way it stands now, you're not going to be able to report out March 17 to the city commission. You've already reported to the public. If you report something different to the city commission, that's not fair to the public."

Frank couldn't be at that meeting. I'm on the phone with him. This is now at 10:30 at night. I have a two-hour drive back. We're on the phone the whole time. Anyway, between the two of us, we were talking about what good work the task force had done. It would just be a shame to lose all the stuff that they had come to agreement on just because of the one issue of culling. Frank and I composed a letter to send back to the task force to say we hoped that they would not give up. We praised them for all the good work they had done and what they had come to agreement on, and said that we hoped that they wouldn't allow everything to fall apart.

The task force then decided to meet on their own. Again, they were very, very split. They did agree that they could go forward with what they agreed upon and that they would just tell the commissioners that they couldn't come up with any concrete recommendation on culling other than the triggers. Then what we were able to do was also put together what was called "next steps" that we recommended to the city commission, where there would need to be some more research done and some different things like that.

They ended up reporting out on March 17. We thought that there would be people from the public who were going to protest this, but we just couldn't believe it. It ended up being a unanimous vote from the city commission to accept what the public task force had come up with, with the idea that the city commission would have to make the ultimate decisions on the culling.

As a result of all of that, there have been some really good things that have happened. We had some impact. There were 15 Boy Scouts who established two deer enclosures. That was one of the recommendations. There was an area school class monitoring the vegetation regrowth. That was a task force recommendation. There were deer resistant plants for homeowners, bulletins developed by Extension for use in Grand Haven and other places. We shared the work that was going on, too, with the annual Michigan Municipal Administrators meeting because they were real interested in it.

The time clock moves forward: now we're in 2009. Last fall there were grumblings again—too many deer; there's got to be culling. It's that culling thing. The city commissioners had some sharpshooters come in and do that. That brought the opposing people back together. People who were against the deer culling formed a group that included a person who had been on the task force. They called it Defenders of Urban Wildlife. I think, just maybe because of the process that Frank and I had used and the way we worked with the group, this group, Defenders of Urban Wildlife, felt very positive about corresponding with Frank and me on some of the things they were thinking of doing. One of the things they wanted to do we thought was very positive: to bring a person that was a master gardener in to talk more about deer resistant plants and other things that people could do. We just suggested it would be good that they work with the local Extension office, because they have a master gardener coordinator. They did this and it brought high praise from both arenas.

The county Extension director (CED) there ended up doing some testifying without letting the university know. It was all in favor of the culling rather than keeping a more neutral position. Extension usually tries to work with both sides. Oh boy! Then things started hitting the paper. Long story short, it was the Extension director in that county who kind of stirred things up again.

The university finally put a gag order on the CED. That's when this public group actually was doing some positive things. We gave them a small grant, asked them to work with the Extension office, and they did and brought in a speaker. It was very positive. It's interesting how we sometimes view expertise in something: here we ended up having a person with the university say, "Well, I know the answer and this is what you should do," rather than allowing people to work through things and come up with a decision.

Frank and I thought it was done back in March of 2008. Then it sort of kept rising up a little bit. It was fairly positive until our local faculty person happened to get involved. I think things have smoothed down a little bit now. It seems the issue of culling kind of bubbles underneath the surface and has been a residual issue for this community, while, in a lot of ways, it's kind of been addressed through the different public forums and the work that's been done thus far.

The city commissioners really need to be commended for even going with a public task force. They could have just made decisions on their own. They took the risk of going with a public task force, of allowing public forums to happen and go with that, and then to really listen to the recommendation. They did move forward with many of the recommendations. They did implement those. With the culling, at least they are doing more of the research that was recommended. They are doing deer counts and that type of thing, so they've got more factual information to share with the public regarding the need to cull.

I think because this has been in the public eye, the public is more tolerant of the issue. I think more people realize that, yes, culling is necessary. Still, people are kind of watching. The commissioners haven't gone crazy and just killed hundreds and hundreds of deer. They've done it very methodically. It's an issue until they really get it under control, which is going to take a number of years. It's still going to probably raise its head every now and then.

The positive thing is that the city of Ferrysburg called the university thinking that they might want us to work with them a little bit. Obviously, surrounding municipalities are seeing that even though it's controversial, there was a lot of good that did come out. There are a lot of things that are being implemented. Some of it is research stuff with the plantings and all of that, so that they can have more factual information for later on.

Who knows what will happen? It's very controversial. It's a huge issue in the whole state of Michigan. Right now I swear you can't drive anywhere without seeing deer. I saw two deer this morning. You just have to be really,

really careful. We are way overpopulated with deer. It's not just the community of Grand Haven. It's other communities that are having to deal with this issue also. If they can learn a little bit from what's happened in Grand Haven and there are some things they can apply in their communities, that's great.

Reflections

Do I feel that the way the community of Grand Haven—the government, citizens, experts, everybody—was involved is a replicable model for other communities? Is Grand Haven unique in the way that they tried to deal with this and continue to do so? I think a lot of the aspects of what they did could be replicated in another community. I'm always cautious because to me, every community is unique. I think there may be aspects of what we did in Grand Haven that would apply very well to another area. I would never tell somebody to say, "Oh, do it exactly this way." I think sometimes people are looking for that. "We're just going to do step one, two, and three." I really caution them because I think you might be able to use step three, but none of the other steps.

Communities really need to talk about their situation. A lot of times they'd rather just take what they did over in this other community and just try to plop it into their community without allowing citizens to talk about what's happening. I think, yeah, there are a lot of parts that could be replicated in another community. But I would caution that community to really talk about what it is they really want to do. That's why we're not saying there are models. We're working with situations. There are some results and impacts that came out of working with this situation. Perhaps some of these ideas you can use over here and then add to it or subtract or whatever. I think that's the way it needs to be presented.

I would say the critical moment, when I wasn't sure whether the community would actually be able to deal with the issues at hand, or just walk away and say, "this is too hard," was when the one individual went to the paper with the op-ed. That was huge. The trust level was broken. It was almost like everybody was just going to walk away. That was a moment where we felt like, "Oh, well, this is great. It's our first experiment, and it's just going to fall on its face." We thought, "Well, that's part of the learning experience."

Frank and I really put our hearts into the letter we wrote in response. We had started really to get to know these people. We also were privy to the personalities of the different individuals on that task force. We were seeing some people really stepping up in leadership roles. Both of us were like, "They've worked so hard." They genuinely were doing the give and take, back and forth. We hated to see the whole thing just drop, because they did actually agree on the majority of things.

I would say it's so critical in the beginning that you take it slow. Gradually, there is trust. I've done a lot of work in trust development. They had built trust in Grand Haven, but it was fragile trust, because they didn't know each other that well. But they were feeling really comfortable with each other. Then when the one person went public without saying anything to anybody, it was like, "We can't trust her. What's she going to say next to the public?"

I think that was a huge moment right there. That was probably the biggest moment. Then one other one was when they couldn't agree on the culling part. On that, there were a couple of people that were just wanting to plow ahead no matter what. Thank goodness they agreed to disagree. They added an addendum to the report that they gave the commissioners. It said that culling was not totally agreed upon by the task force. The fact that they then were able to respect each other at least enough to come back together—we didn't know whether they would or not—to talk and then to agree to disagree on the culling but to move forward with the other good work that they had done, that was huge.

I've done a lot of facilitating, and I think for me it's a lot different from teaching a class and addressing community issues or issue framing or whatever. This is real application. Part of me says I was pulling not only from my public deliberation skills, but from a lot of the facilitation skills that I've honed over the years. Your stomach is churning because it's almost like, "Okay, we want to make this work," but you have to keep in the back of your mind it's the people first. It's their issue. The most we can do is help raise those questions and keep them talking and moving along.

I think you have to not be afraid that things may be falling apart. Sometimes things fall apart. Then maybe there's an incubation time. Then they come back together, and things go well. It's sort of stormy. Local situations are messy. It's tough when you're dealing with experts or people who perceive themselves as experts to get them to be more down to earth. People are pretty smart if you just allow them to have their say.

What do I walk away with when reflecting on my work with Grand Haven? Well, it just strengthens my belief in citizens really knowing what's best for their communities. To be honest, sometimes it's the public officials that really get in the way. I think the more we can get public officials involving the public, the better the solutions to the situations will be. The problem is that I think too many public officials are frightened of what the public might say or might do or be willing to do. It's a bold step to trust and take a look at what the public would come up with, and implement what they might say. It ends up being a win-win situation. I guess that's what I would say.

Interview conducted by Timothy J. Shaffer

A Historical Note

Farmer Discussion Groups, Citizen-Centered Politics, and Cooperative Extension

by Timothy J. Shaffer

The prophets speak of things not happening "until the fullness of time thereof." I am sure the time has come when there is a demand for a great discussion movement on the part of the citizens. The question is, do the educational agencies have the statesmanship, the understanding, and the technique to make this a great vitalizing movement in democracy at the present time?[1]

M. L. Wilson, Undersecretary
US Department of Agriculture, 1936

In reading these profiles, one might assume that deliberative approaches to public problems are a new way to engage citizens in understanding and addressing shared challenges. Yet significantly, there are historical precedents for this approach, with land-grant universities and Cooperative Extension serving not only as partners in such work, but also as central actors. This chapter focuses on a little-known initiative that is an important element of the prophetic narrative about what institutions, such as Extension, *should* be doing in our democratic society.[2] It fleshes out in some detail an historical example of a partnership between the United States Department of Agriculture (USDA) and Extension that looked to rural communities as places to cultivate democratic habits which would help citizens understand and respond to the changes taking place during the mid-1930s and early 1940s. This particular chapter of Extension's history offers a look into an effort designed to help foster democratic discussions by training Extension professionals to organize and convene them.[3]

EXPERIMENTING WITH DISCUSSION IN THE NEW DEAL

"Perhaps we haven't given enough attention to the farmer as a citizen," USDA assistant secretary M. L. Wilson told government and university administrators gathered in Washington, DC, in February 1935. Together, they were exploring the possibility of creating a new adult education program based on discussion methods that would reach people in rural communities across the country through the existing network of Cooperative Extension agents.[4]

Instead of just using a top-down technical approach to address issues as might be expected from a government agency in the Great Depression, Wilson, USDA secretary Henry A. Wallace, and others chose to support community-based adult education which emphasized the importance of citizens discussing issues together.[5] These administrators sought to encourage a kind of democracy in which citizens were willing and able to identify and articulate their interests, beliefs, and values alongside neighbors and colleagues. In short, what these administrators were attempting to cultivate was a kind of democracy in which people were willing to talk, listen, and learn with and from others.

What they helped create was a program called Program Study and Discussion (PSD), first as a Section in the Agricultural Adjustment Administration and later in the Bureau of Agricultural Economics and elevated to a Division, both within the USDA. The PSD's work encompassed two related programs: discussion groups that were originally intended to be organized by local Extension agents with rural men and women, and schools of philosophy for Extension workers—typically three- or four-day continuing education programs organized by USDA staff that included speakers from many prestigious universities with diverse scholarly interests and backgrounds. The schools were originally for Extension agents but quickly expanded to serve other community leaders interested in thinking about the "farm problem" more broadly than as an economic issue.[6]

From 1935 until the PSD was closed in 1946, the unit produced and distributed millions of copies of discussion guides on more than 40 subjects, although groups were encouraged to address topics well beyond those outlined in the government pamphlets and to develop their own resources for group discussion.[7] The PSD also prepared materials for how to organize and lead group discussions.[8] Wide-ranging discussion guides explored issues, such as differences between how urban and rural people lived, taxes, environmental concerns, and agricultural policy.

Final numbers suggest that more than 3 million rural men and women participated in discussion groups annually, tens of thousands of discussion leaders were trained, and more than 150 Schools of Philosophy attracted more than 50,000 Extension workers and other rural community leaders.[9] With a small central staff based in Washington, DC, the PSD engaged communities across the country. Ultimately, the program ended because of two major factors: first, World War II shifted priorities to a new set of societal needs; and second, actions taken by the American Farm Bureau Federation, sympathetic supporters in Congress, and some within the land-grant colleges who opposed the work of the Bureau of Agricultural Economics, were successful in reducing and defunding it.[10] Among other things, those who fought to end these programs felt that the type of work the USDA was "supposed" to be doing was to provide the public with statistical information, not engaging farmers in participatory planning and the kind of educational work that defined the PSD.

For this volume and for our concerns about how professionals can join with others with a degree of humility in their approach to public work, there are three key takeaways from this historical period.

EDUCATION AND DISCUSSION AT THE CENTER OF DEMOCRATIC LIFE

The first takeaway is that administrators recognized the importance of education and discussion in a democracy and chose to do something about it. Group discussion offered an explicit opportunity to reconceptualize the relationships among a federal agency, land-grant universities,

Extension agents, and community members by asking Extension professionals to convene people and engage in reflective and critical discussion rather than to simply interact with them as experts. Collaboration and discussion had long been at the heart of Extension's work. C. B. Smith and M. C. Wilson wrote in 1930 about how Extension agents and farming people "together made the analysis of conditions, together selected the outstanding needs, and together made a program to meet those needs."[11] The discussion project took this kind of collaboration a step further, not only encouraging people to do the practical work together, but also to delve deeply into the more philosophical questions facing individuals and communities. *delve deeply into*

Despite the fact that much of the work of the USDA did not rely on citizens discussing and deliberating issues, Wilson, Wallace, Carl F. Taeusch (head of the PSD), and others wanted discussion to be the cornerstone of how the USDA—and other government agencies—approached their work in and with communities. Their vision, it's important to point out, redefined what it meant to be a professional in both government agencies and universities. Wilson wanted continuing education—embodied in group discussion—to be one of the major pillars of agricultural policy.[12]

Jess Gilbert, writing about adult education and discussion as part of the USDA's role during the New Deal, put it this way: "Probably the most unusual innovation of the New Deal USDA aimed to advance democracy through adult or continuing education."[13] He argues that the intention behind these programs was to "expand the views of local and state leaders in both government and society at large."[14] In his study of the USDA's democratic work during this period, Gilbert notes that Wallace and Wilson "understood education as a promising way to foster democratic citizenship and foment social change." These government administrators "counted themselves among a 'great democratic movement' that put continuing education at its core."[15]

These efforts were not just another set of programs of the New Deal. They were ventures to engage people in ways that were less transactional than the routine Extension practices of disseminating information and encouraging the adoption of certain methods in agriculture and home economics. Instead, group discussion was seen as foundational to democratic society and Extension was the institution charged with the task of bolstering democratic discourse through education.[16] Paul L. Vogt, one of the staff members of the PSD would note, "The United States Department of Agriculture is glad to help in this movement as a significant part of a national rural civic educational movement." Vogt stated that this educational work was "not a teaching process in the usual sense of the term, but a drawing out and sharing process, such as characterizes ordinary conversation." Education was embodied through conversations between citizens, tapping into their lived experiences. In short, they recognized the importance of everyday talk.[17]   *lived experience*

The efforts of administrators shaping the PSD embodied a public philosophy—the political theory implicit in one's practice—committed to democracy as a way of life rather than limiting "democracy" to periodic voting and an otherwise passive role for citizens. As PSD director Taeusch put it, "The problem of educating the voter to take an intelligent part in elections has long been recognized as paramount in a democracy. But we are now rapidly coming to see that this objective is too limited. Of perhaps even greater importance is the problem of educating the administrator, private as well as public, potential as well as actual."[18]

While the Dust Bowl was a reality for many rural Americans, eroding farmland was not the only loss they suffered during that time. As one author put it, "Erosion of the soil in which democracy can grow has also taken place at an accelerating rate."[19] Supporting attempts to cultivate a deeper knowledge about agricultural problems, Wilson, Wallace, Taeusch and others envisioned the USDA helping address problems in democracy by attempting to wrestle with the problems of democracy.[20]

What these leaders envisioned was not novel. In fact, much of what they wanted to create—spaces for citizens to engage and learn with and from one another—was built on previous generations of work.[21] One of Secretary Wallace's first speeches in 1933 was called "A Declaration of Interdependence." He spoke about the desperate situation facing farmers as well as the many urban dwellers who had turned to abandoned farms with the hope of making a future for themselves. What was needed was "a mental adjustment, a willing reversal, of driving, pioneer opportunism and ungoverned *laissez-faire*. The ungoverned push of rugged individualism perhaps had an economic justification in the days when we had all the West to surge upon and conquer; but this country has filled up now, and grown up."[22] The vision for the USDA as a whole was to engage people as meaningful civic actors in relationship with other citizens, not simply recipients of government services.

Wilson shared many views with Wallace, among them that Americans needed to look beyond economics as the measure for understanding issues.[23] In a striking statement, Wilson, trained as an agricultural economist, expressed his views about the complexity of issues and why we must think broadly about even a narrowly defined issue:

> I have always believed that no single specialist or expert, nor any single body of scientific knowledge, can ever deal adequately with even a relatively small and apparently detached agricultural problem. I believe that when, for instance, we have a farm problem that seems on the surface to be wholly an economic matter, we may safely take it for granted that the economic problem is interwoven with factors that are political, sociological, psychological, philosophical, and even religious. And we should realize that any solution or policy that is decided upon is bound to have effects upon human life and conduct that none but philosophy and religion openly profess to judge. Economic wisdom alone, therefore, is not enough for proper consideration of agricultural problems that by common consent are defined as economic problems. We cannot escape getting involved in questions of moral, philosophical, and spiritual values whenever we touch upon any social problem.[24]

In 1940, Wilson wrote that he was convinced the problems of rural life would not be solved by "present-day social science disciplines," but rather through a cultural approach "attempting to get an integrated view of life as it flows along."[25] Democracy was shaped by value-laden questions, and citizens needed to turn to one another, and not simply to experts, for wisdom and discussion about what should be done. He believed issues

cornerstone, pillars

needed to be named and framed as complex problems, even when they appeared to be simple.[26] Education—through discussion with others— was a powerful way for individuals to more fully understand the intercon- nected realities of their world. In a time when fundamental questions about democracy's future were up for debate, the PSD cultivated space for thoughtful discussion about democratic life.

DEMOCRACY IN PRACTICE

The second key takeaway is that we cannot simply talk about democ- racy but must also commit to the development and utilization of resources to encourage and support democratic discussion. Wilson stressed that the "time [was] ripe for purposeful discussion about the big questions of future agricultural policies," in large part because they lived in a transi- tional time increasingly influenced by "science and the machine." For him, these changes did not simply mean that farmers would be using mechanical tractors. Rather, the machine-age ideology challenged the belief that ordi- nary people could comprehend the issues of the day and have meaningful roles in shaping society. As he stated emphatically: "Free and full discussion is the archstone of democracy." Rural people did not need to be preached at. Instead, they should be active participants in creating their future. This was not necessarily new to Extension, "but there [had] never been a better opportunity or a greater need for using it as a means of stimulating the flow of pro and con thought," Wilson argued.[27]

Under Wallace's leadership, the agricultural sciences were ideally complemented by considerations about the broader social and philosoph- ical implications of agricultural policy. USDA leaders sought to broaden thinking about agricultural policy and rural issues. Discussion groups and schools of philosophy were two of the ways the USDA engaged citizens in educational work around complex, public problems. For Wallace, Wilson, and Taeusch, education was deeply influential in the development of one's values and philosophy about life. Education enabled people to think and act differently, and if the USDA could support that process, it was doing an important aspect of its work for rural Americans.

Discussion groups offered facilitators an opportunity to use group discussion methods as a way to contribute to the "enlightenment of the public and to the civic vitality of the community." This was accomplished, ideally, in two ways: (1) "by affording an opportunity to its citizens to become active participants in public affairs instead of being mere passive recipients of radio programs, speeches, lectures, newspaper articles, and the like, and (2) by opening national problems to serious public consideration. This grounding of local, regional, and national issues and policies in the minds of the people is indispensable to the functioning of a democracy."[28]

Extension leaders designated agents in their states to lead training and educational efforts.[29] Additionally, resources were made available to those who would serve as discussion group leaders free of charge. If agents or others needed discussion materials, they simply wrote to the PSD in Washington. These documents offered suggestions on how to organize and convene group discussions, importantly making distinctions between panels, forums, and discussion groups (see Figure 1). In what might be referred to in today's language as "best practices," the guides offered

Figure 1: Methodological Materials Published by USDA

D-1.	Discussion: A Brief Guide to Methods [1935]
D-2.	How to Organize and Conduct County Forums [1935] and Suggestions for County Extension Workers on Forum and Discussion Groups (Mimeographed)
D-3.	What is the Discussion Leader's Job? [1937]
D-4.	Group Discussion and Its Techniques [1942]
D-5.	Organization of Groups for Discussion and Action [1942]
DN-1.	Suggestions for Discussion Group Members
DN-2.	Suggestions for Group Discussion Leaders
DN-3.	Suggestions for County Extension Workers on Forum and Discussion Groups
DN-4.	Suggestions for Panel Discussions

Source: J. Gilbert, *Planning Democracy: Agrarian Intellectuals and the Intended New Deal* (NewHaven, CT: Yale University Press, 2015), 261.

insight into the practical steps for leading group discussions that were inclusive and participatory.[30]

When we look at these efforts by the USDA and Extension, we find democracy in practice. Wallace, Wilson, and Taeusch were not simply romantics longing for a bygone era of the New England town hall meeting, although they sought to build on this democratic tradition.[31] The world was rapidly changing, and their response was to develop initiatives that would strengthen citizen-centered democracy. This cut against the grain of many descriptions of the New Deal as a period of an increasingly powerful federal government that embraced only bureaucratic and technocratic approaches to public problems. Explicitly, this continuing education program was rooted in the state- and county-based Extension services rather than in the federal government.[32]

Extension agents in North Carolina (1 of 10 states that piloted discussion groups in 1935) worked with communities in which participants expressed appreciation for the opportunity to have these discussions.[33] Just months after the idea of group discussion got off the ground, the local newspaper in New Bern, North Carolina, ran an article entitled, "Discussion Plan Gains Favor with County's Farmers." The story captured the strong interest of rural people in opportunities to participate with their neighbors in civic discussions. One farmer told an Extension agent that instead of having discussions lasting six or seven weeks, they ought to be lasting for six or seven years. The hope was, according to the Extension agent involved, that the discussions being held in various communities might be continued indefinitely. Another participant suggested that "what is needed in every county is a 'William Green' to speak for the little man, who can't hold his own with the larger landowners who have become established." This comment elicited a give-and-take about the role of government, the role of the individual, and the feasibility of continuing to farm when it did not seem to be economically viable.[34] The experiments in states, such as North Carolina, gave the USDA and Extension leadership enough justification to support this initiative. By the following January, 30 states supported discussion groups, with the number expanding to more than 40 a few years later.[35]

As can be seen by the plan shown in Figure 2, Oklahoma Extension had fully embraced the idea of the discussions since their involvement as a test site in 1935. The plan for organizing and setting up group discussions at the local, county, and state levels in diverse settings and organizations relied on Extension as the connective thread, running from national work around group discussion all the way down to local civic organizations, such as parent-teacher associations and 4-H clubs.

In a document entitled "Suggestions to County Agricultural Extension Agents for Organizing and Setting Up County and Local Discussion Groups," state group discussion leader John M. White of Oklahoma Agricultural and Mechanical College noted that county agents were to serve as discussion leaders, but they were to collaborate with community members. The role of the agent was to work closely with a community leader to determine in which settings discussion might be profitable and useful. This approach encouraged Extension to partner and collaborate with others in identifying additional community members and organizations to be engaged in discussion about issues of importance to them.[36] Furthermore, the PSD expressed the hope that citizens would organize and convene themselves, utilizing the resources published by the USDA as well as materials from libraries, newspapers, speeches, and specialists like Extension agents.[37]

Other states, such as Michigan, sought to integrate discussion methods into existing Extension work in ways similar to those employed in Oklahoma. Michigan State College appointed a county Extension agent, William F. Johnston, to the position of State Leader of Discussion Groups. He assumed this role on January 1, 1936.[38] In his first monthly report, Johnston wrote that Farm Bureaus had "a decided interest" in discussion methods and saw opportunities for using them within their own organizations. A number of county agents across Michigan expressed interest in this new method, meeting with Johnston multiple times to determine how to move forward with their respective groups and how to develop local leadership. "I am working on the principle that the County Agent is the keystone, and it will probably take some time for him to ascertain what success he will have in enrolling local leaders," Johnston wrote.[39]

Figure 2: Plan for Organizing and Setting Up State, County, and Local Discussion Group Project

EXTENSION

NATIONAL DIRECTOR - GROUP DISCUSSION PROJECT

M. L. Wilson, National Director
Agricultural Extension Service
U. S. Department of Agriculture
Washington, D. C.

STATE DIRECTOR - GROUP DISCUSSION PROJECT

E. E. Scholl, State Director
Agricultural Extension Service
A. & M. College
Stillwater, Oklahoma

STATE CO-DIRECTORS - GROUP DISCUSSION PROJECT

| AAA
FSA
BAE
SCS
REA | Dir. Exp.
Station
FCA | LUP
Committees
Vocational
Agriculture
State HDA | Councils of
Defense
Indian
Service
4-H | Farners'
Union
Others | Co-ops
State
Grange
Others | Federation of
Churches |

STATE DISCUSSION LEADER

John M. White
Agricultural Extension Service
A. & M. College
Stillwater, Oklahoma

COUNTY GROUP DISCUSSION LEADERS

County Agriculture Extension Agents

CO-COUNTY GROUP DISCUSSION LEADERS

| LUP Com.
AAA
FSA
BAE
SCS
REA | Councils
of Defense
Dir. Exp.
Station
FCA | Vocational
Agriculture
State HDA | Schools
Indian
Service
4-H | Farners'
Union
Others | Co-ops
State
Grange
Others | Federation
of Churches
Others |

OPEN FIELD LOCAL ORGANIZATIONS THAT MAY BE INTERESTED

| LUP Committees
Farm Organization
Agri. Committees
Schools
Churches
Others | Civic Organizations
P.T.A.'s
Cooperative
Associations
Others | H.D.A. Clubs
4-H Clubs
F.F.A.
Councils of Defense
Others | Congenial Groups
City or Rural
Community Clubs
Others |

Figure 2: Reproduced by permission of Presidents' Papers Collection, Special Collections & University Archives, Oklahoma State University Libraries. 1970-005. 30, Folder 11: Extension Division - Correspondence 1941-1943.

In the neighboring state of Ohio, the goal was to "make . . . rural leaders conscious of the value of the discussion method," according to J. P. Schmidt, supervisor of farmers' institutes at Ohio State University.[40] The approach employed in Ohio was to involve a wide range of organizations—the Grange, Farm Bureau, 4-H clubs, college faculty, county planning committees, community adult schools, rural ministers' summer schools, and vocational agricultural departments—in learning about the benefit of discussion and to determine how best to use the method in their diverse settings.

In the pamphlet published by the PSD called, *What Is the Discussion Leader's Job?* the citizen-centered approach to discussion groups was made clear as an alternative to simply relying on experts to identify and address issues. Under the subheading "When Is Discussion Most Helpful?" the diverse approaches to helping people understand public issues were identified—lectures, demonstrations, debates—and appropriateness for various environments was acknowledged. But what made discussion different from these other approaches was that discussion, "offers to members of the group opportunities to state a problem in their own terms and use their own resources toward a solution." The pamphlet continued: "The discussion method is primarily desirable as a means of solving problems about which some information is already available and on which executive action is still in the future, but concerning which active interest and divergent views exist in the community."[41] Discussion ideally built on knowledge about issues, but it gave space for citizens to contribute to that shared understanding, as well as to weigh the tensions and trade-offs that come with any public decision. Additionally, the pamphlet noted that there were individual and community benefits to engaging in discussion:

- **For the individual:** In addition to a desire to join in the give-and-take of forming opinion, a good many people relish the discussion process because it disciplines both their thinking and their social behavior. Gaining skill in analyzing the main features of a point of view, and presenting them clearly, attractively, and briefly; learning to listen to and think through divergent views and cooperating in finding common ground between them; the excitement of finding new facts following an opening up of issues, all give a sense of personal growth which participants appreciate keenly.

- **For the community:** Where public issues are the subject of lively discussion, people are citizens in fact as well as in name. The give-and-take helps them put on mental muscle, and develops both leaders and the type of intelligent follower who gives representative government something to represent. Unless the interests of the people are locally made known, and unless policies for furthering those interests are locally worked out, the action of economic events will force the making of policy by the central government. Where local provision is made for the development of policy, problems are foreseen and examined before they reach the stage of being crises, before it is necessary to plunge into action without much previous exploration of the problem and without previous achievement of agreement by the people. This is working democracy.[42]

As the material amply reflected, the benefits were both individual and collective, rooted in a sense of being part of a democratic society that took seriously the need for citizens not only to be educated but also to actively participate in political life. The commitment of Extension in states like North Carolina, Michigan, Ohio, and Oklahoma to designating statewide discussion coordinators made it possible for group discussion to flourish, or at least to be tried out by populations that may not otherwise have done so. But for many reasons, the efforts to enliven rural communities through discussion about a range of topics were limited.

PUSHBACK AND DECLINE

The third takeaway of this historical case is the acknowledgement that commitment by key leaders does not necessarily translate into adoption by members of the broader organization. For all the time spent on the project through the establishment of statewide discussion leaders in Extension, farm men and women had their own priorities and so did institutions like land-grant universities and, more specifically, Extension. Participation in discussion groups had less priority than some of their more pressing concerns and interests, especially as the abysmal economic climate of the mid-1930s dragged on. And when concerns shifted to foreign threats, in the 1940s, interest in discussion about diverse topics gave way to practical concerns about how to increase production for a world at war.

Additionally, despite the USDA's firmly stated position against advocating for particular views on issues, people continued to be wary of something that seemed so political in nature coming from the federal government and state universities. William Johnston from Michigan acknowledged this:

> I seem to detect a covert suspicion that there are political angles to the project, and that it will be better to wait until the heat of the election campaign has subsided; that is to say leaders seem to fear that they will have a hard time keeping these things down in their groups. So I conclude it will require patience, and constant, genial, and good natured pecking to put this project over.[43]

Some people who participated in discussions objected to the USDA materials because "there [wasn't] any answer in the back of the book." "Nowhere do these pamphlets try to say what the 'right' answer to each question is," an article in *Wallaces' Farmer* stated. "Instead, they merely say that there are half a dozen answers, supported by certain evidence. It is up to the farm groups to go over the various arguments and try to figure out how much sense there is in each of them," the article continued. In a variety of contexts, citizens had grown accustomed to doing what experts suggested and while deliberative discussion offered an alternative for participants to come to their own conclusions, this was not necessarily what they wanted to do.[44]

There were challenges to overcoming the perceived political nature of democratic discussions as well as to changing how people related to experts, but another major hurdle for this work came from Extension agents themselves. As noted in the introduction, Gladys L. Baker's 1939 study on Extension highlighted the resistance and hesitation many agents had about the discussion efforts that were receiving so much attention from USDA administrators.[45]

Department administrators were deeply committed to infusing as many facets of the department as possible with democratic discussion methods.[46] In a memorandum to USDA staff about how departmental staff and colleagues should work alongside farmers in tackling the amorphous "farm problem," Secretary Wallace believed local land-use planning— one of the action programs developed alongside group discussion—was a way for national-level agricultural policy to be shaped, in part, by actions taken by farmers in their own communities in conversation with others.[47]

But Extension agents did not necessarily share this view. A letter from C. V. Ballard, State Leader of County Agents at Michigan State College, to a PSD staff member about the use of discussion included praise for the USDA's effort but also concern about the widespread use of group discussion as a teaching method by Extension agents: "To ask Extension workers who have been trained in the lecture method of teaching to suddenly change to the group discussion method is something like asking the cheering section to listen to the applause."[48] Repeated opportunities for Extension agents to be introduced to the benefits of discussion did not necessarily translate into adoption. Michigan communities remained actively engaged with discussion group work, although it would continue to be seen as a marginal effort when compared with the more traditional work of Extension and Michigan State overall.[49]

In many ways, it was this reframing of the "farm problem" from an economic or technical problem to a more complex issue that changed the role and relationship between government agencies, Extension, the Farm Bureau, and citizens that helped end this period of democratic experimentation. As is often the case still today, Extension agents were trained in their respective fields and areas of expertise to know what to do when and how; they did not necessarily have the training, skills, or interest to facilitate discussions that were exploratory and open-ended.

Finally, there were also larger societal shifts in the United States, notably the move away from face-to-face forums to alternatives for entertainment and policy discussion through radio programs, such as *America's Town Meeting on the Air*. Writing about the decline of another forum movement

↓ Putnam also thinks this way

from the period, Christopher Loss noted, "The coming television age offered a powerful alternative to the face-to-face give-and-take of the forum model, irrevocably changing the manner in which most Americans received news and participated in democratic deliberation." Forums "died peaceful deaths from lack of interest," in the words of William Keith and Paula Cossart.[50] While the PSD was able to morph itself in response to World War II, producing discussion guides with titles such as, "Let's Talk about When Joe Comes Home and Comes Back to the Farm," people and the government moved on.[51]

CONCLUSION

The existence of the PSD between 1935 and 1946 challenges popular histories of the land-grant university and the Extension system. By creating spaces for citizens to learn from one another, deliberate, and (in partnership with the USDA's more explicit action programs such as land-use planning) to act, Wallace, Wilson, and others sought to cultivate a more democratic approach to understanding and addressing public problems. Framing the most pressing agricultural issues as *questions for citizens to answer and act on themselves* serves as a reminder of the attempts made to strengthen democracy while simultaneously seeking to address public problems.

Based on a public philosophy committed to education as an essential element of democracy and to the concept that citizens should be active participants and contributors to public life, Wallace, Wilson, Taeusch, and the PSD sought to remake and strengthen democracy by practicing democracy. The significant challenge to realizing this, however, was the pushback from within Extension and the shifting societal needs in response to World War II. There were competing views of how Extension professionals should engage in their work and what their *work* was.

Look back to Carmen DeRusha's comments earlier in this book. She speaks about her work and identity in Extension as something she was able to shape: "I was lucky enough to be given a job concept, not a job description, so I created my own identity. Let's put it that way. My identity was created based on the mission of the organization, not based on the methods or the structure of the system." In a similar way, the Extension professionals charged with developing discussion groups in the mid-1930s and early 1940s had a comparable experience when it came to aligning their identities and roles with a commitment to the mission of Extension—helping cultivate in people a sense that they were necessary contributors to democratic life.

While resources were made widely and freely available, much of the work connected to discussion groups was rooted in Extension agents' understanding of how it aligned with their own positions and identities. Michigan Extension agent William Johnston came to the field of democratic group discussion without a sense of what this pedagogical approach meant for him. Nevertheless, he opened himself to learning about the topic from diverse sources.[52] Over time, he came to embrace the possibilities of discussion for Extension and how it could create more opportunities for rural people to engage one another around issues of shared concern. But the work was about more than solving problems. M. L. Wilson was hopeful that education through group discussion would be both "a means and . . . an end" to a more vibrant democracy. Thus, we can view this chapter in Extension history not as a failed venture, but as a prophetic story that can serve as a foundational narrative supporting the commitments of those profiled in this book who are building on, and further developing, an important element of the Extension story—whether they were previously aware of this earlier chapter or not.

It is important to understand and reclaim periods in the past that help us imagine and articulate what it means to live public-spirited lives that shine a light on the knowledge and agency of citizens. Institutions like universities and federal bureaucracies are often viewed as being out of touch with democratic life and active citizenship. Yet, as this chapter reveals, we can uncover and reclaim forgotten stories that offer alternative narratives about the role that professionals in Extension had in fostering citizen-centered politics in response to public problems. Additionally, by drawing on the rich work by university faculty and Extension professionals both yesterday and today, we can look toward Extension's future by acknowledging that democracy is something made anew in every generation and that we have a role to play.

ENDNOTES

[1]   M. L. Wilson, "Education for Democracy," in *Education for Democracy: Proceedings of the Nineteenth American Country Life Conference*, Kalamazoo, Michigan, August 10-13, 1936, edited by Benson Y. Landis (Chicago; New York: The University of Chicago Press; American Country Life Association, 1937), 14.

[2]   On the role of such institutions, see Timothy J. Shaffer, "Looking Beyond Our Recent Past," *National Civic Review 105*, no. 3 (2016); "Institutions Supporting Democratic Communication among Citizens," *National Civic Review* 106, no. 1 (2017).

[3]   For more on this topic, see Jess Gilbert, *Planning Democracy: Agrarian Intellectuals and the Intended New Deal* (New Haven, CT: Yale University Press, 2015); Timothy J. Shaffer, "What Should You and I Do? Lessons for Civic Studies from Deliberative Politics in the New Deal," *The Good Society* 22, no. 2 (2013); "Cultivating Deliberative Democracy through Adult Civic Education: The Ideas and Work That Shaped Farmer Discussion Groups and Schools of Philosophy in the New Deal Department of Agriculture, Land-Grant Universities, and Cooperative Extension Service" (Cornell University, 2014); T. J. Shaffer, "Thinking Beyond Food and Fiber: Public Dialogue and Deliberation in the New Deal Department of Agriculture," in *The Intersection of Food and Public Health: Examining Current Challenges and Solutions in Policy and Politics*, edited by A.B. Hoflund, J. Jones, and M. C. Pautz (New York: Routledge, 2018), 307-326; "Supporting the 'Archstone of Democracy': Cooperative Extension's Experiment with Deliberative Group Discussion," *Journal of Extension*, 55(5), Article 5FEA1, available at: https://joe.org/joe/2017october/a2011.php.

[4]   United States Department of Agriculture, *Preliminary Report of the Forum and Discussion Group Project*, United States Department of Agriculture, 1934-1935 (n.p.: United States Department of Agriculture, 1935), 5.

[5]   On the role of democratic planning, see Gilbert, *Planning Democracy*.

[6]   While both of these programs were central to the work of the PSD, the focus of this chapter is on discussion groups. For more on Schools of Philosophy, see Gilbert, *Planning Democracy*, 156-166; Andrew Jewett, "The Social Sciences, Philosophy, and the Cultural Turn in the 1930s USDA," *Journal of the History of the Behavioral Sciences* 49, no. 4 (2013); Shaffer, "What Should You and I Do?"; "Cultivating Deliberative Democracy through Adult Civic Education."; Carl F. Taeusch, *Report on the Schools of Philosophy for Agricultural Leaders* (Washington, DC: United States Department of Agriculture; Bureau of Agricultural Economics, 1941); "Schools of Philosophy," *Agricultural Library Notes* 16, no. 10 (1941); Shaffer, "Thinking Beyond Food and Fiber: Public Dialogue and Deliberation in the New Deal Department of Agriculture."; "Supporting the 'Archstone of Democracy': Cooperative Extension's Experiment with Deliberative Group Discussion in the New Deal."

7   For a complete list of discussion materials produced, see Gilbert, *Planning Democracy*, 261-263.

8   For methodological materials, see Figure 1.

9   Carl F. Taeusch, "Freedom of Assembly," *Ethics* 63, no. 1 (1952): 41; "Division Activities—February, 1943," in *Record Group* 83 (Box 535: Entry 19, Folder "Division of Program Study and Discussion," 1943); David Lachman, "Democratic Ideology and Agricultural Policy 'Program Study and Discussion' in the U.S. Department of Agriculture, 1934-1946" (Master's Thesis, University of Wisconsin - Madison, 1991), 50; Gilbert, *Planning Democracy*, 142; Shaffer, "What Should You and I Do?" 141; "Cultivating Deliberative Democracy through Adult Civic Education"; Paul L. Vogt, "Study Clubs and Citizenship," *Mountain Life and Work* 15, no. 4 (1940): 6; A. Drummond Jones (1941); Farmer Discussion Is Adult Education, *Adult Education Bulletin*, 5(4): 121-125.

10   Richard S. Kirkendall, *Social Scientists and Farm Politics in the Age of Roosevelt* (Columbia: University of Missouri Press, 1966), 195-261; Gilbert, *Planning Democracy*, 238-260.

11   C. B. Smith and M. C. Wilson, *The Agricultural Extension System of the United States* (New York: John Wiley & Sons, 1930), 132.

12   Gilbert, *Planning Democracy*, 146, 178.

13   Ibid., 142.

14   Jess Gilbert, "Low Modernism and the Agrarian New Deal," in *Fighting for the Farm: Rural America Transformed*, edited by Jane Adams (Philadelphia: University of Pennsylvania Press, 2003), 136.

15   Gilbert, *Planning Democracy*, 143.

16   Shaffer, "Supporting the 'Archstone of Democracy.'"

17   P. L. Vogt, Study Clubs and Citizenship, *Mountain Life and Work*, 15(4) (1940): 6, 7.

18   C. F. Taeusch, "Schools of Philosophy for Farmers," in *Farmers in a Changing World*, edited by G. Hambidge (Washington, DC: US Government Printing Office, 1940), 1113.

19   F. F. Elliott, "We, the People ..." *Land Policy Review* 2, no. 3 (1939): 2.

20   On this distinction, see Mathews, *The Ecology of Democracy*.

21   See Scott J. Peters, *Changing the Story About Higher Education's Public Purposes and Work: Land-Grants, Liberty, and the Little Country Theater* (Ann Arbor, MI: Imagining America [Foreseeable Futures Position Paper #6, published by Imagining America: Artists and Scholars in Public Life], 2007); Scott J. Peters, "Storying and Restorying the Land-Grant System," in *The Land-Grant Colleges and the Reshaping of American Higher Education*, edited by Roger L. Geiger and Nathan M. Sorber (New Brunswick, NJ: Transaction Publishers, 2013).

22   Henry A. Wallace, *Democracy Reborn: Selected from Public Papers and Edited with an Introduction and Notes by Russell Lord* (New York: Reynal & Hitchcock, 1944), 44-45.

23   Henry A. Wallace, "We Are More Than Economic Men," *Scribner's Magazine* 96, no. 6 (1934); M. L. Wilson, "Beyond Economics," in *Farmers in a Changing World*, edited by Gove Hambidge (Washington, DC: United States Government Printing Office, 1940).

24   M. L. Wilson, "Patterns of Rural Cultures," in *Agriculture in Modern Life*, edited by O.E. Baker, Ralph Borsodi, and M. L. Wilson (New York: Harper & Brothers Publishers, 1939), 218.

25   M. L. Wilson, "The Democratic Processes and the Formulation of Agricultural Policy," *Social Forces* 19, no. 1 (1940): 11.

26   M. L. Wilson, "Patterns of Rural Cultures," 218; M. L. Wilson, "The New Department of Agriculture," in Address before the Annual Meeting of the Texas Agricultural Workers Association (Fort Worth, TX,1939), 10-11; "Beyond Economics."

27   M. L. Wilson, "Discussion Time Is Here," *Extension Service Review* 6, no. 10 (1935).

28   United States Department of Agriculture, *The Extension Service, and Agricultural Adjustment Administration, Discussion: A Brief Guide to Methods D-1* (Washington, DC: US Government Printing Office, 1935), 1-2.

29   Shaffer, "Supporting the 'Archstone of Democracy': Cooperative Extension's Experiment with Deliberative Group Discussion in the New Deal."

30   United States Department of Agriculture, The Extension Service, and Agricultural Adjustment Administration, *Discussion: A Brief Guide to Methods D-1*; Bureau of Agricultural Economics, *Group Discussion and Its Techniques: A Bibliographical Review* (Washington, DC: US Government Printing Office, 1942); United States Department of Agriculture, The Extension Service, and Agricultural Adjustment Administration, *What Is the Discussion Leader's Job? D-3* (Washington, DC: United States Government Printing Office, 1937).

31   Shaffer, "Institutions Supporting Democratic Communication among Citizens."; "Democracy and Education: Historical Roots of Deliberative Pedagogy," in *Deliberative Pedagogy: Teaching and Learning for Democratic Engagement*, edited by Timothy J. Shaffer, et al. (East Lansing, MI: Michigan State University Press, 2017).

32   Gilbert, *Planning Democracy*, 147.

33   The pilot phase of discussion groups in the spring of 1935 included Iowa, Kansas, Massachusetts, Minnesota, New York, North Carolina, Ohio, Oklahoma, Utah, and Washington.

34   "Discussion Plan Gains Favor with County's Farmers, *Sun Journal*, March 22, 1935," in *Record Group 16* (Box 4: Entry 34, Folder "North Carolina", 1935), The Records of the Office of the Secretary of Agriculture, National Archives.

35   A. Drummond Jones, "Farmers Forming Discussion Groups in More Than 40 States," *Bulletin of the American Library Association* 33, no. 3 (1939): 166.

36   "Plan for Organizing and Setting up State, County and Local Discussion Group Project," in *1970-005* (30, Folder 11: Extension Division—Correspondence 1941-1943, n.d.), OSU Presidents' Papers Collection, Special Collections & University Archives, Oklahoma State University Libraries.

37   Vogt, "Study Clubs and Citizenship," 6.

38   R. J. Baldwin, "Report of Cooperative Extension Work in Agriculture and Home Economics for Year Ending December 31, 1936," University Archives and Historical Collections, Michigan State University, 8.

39   William F. Johnston, "Monthly Narrative Report of Extension Specialist, State Discussion Group Leader, June 1936" in Cooperative Extension Service Records, Box 2219, Folder 41, University Archives and Historical Collections, Michigan State University.

40   "Let Them Talk Says Ohio Leaders Who Use Discussion in Teaching," *Extension Service Review* 7, no. 2 (1936): 17.

41   United States Department of Agriculture, The Extension Service, and Agricultural Adjustment Administration, *What Is the Discussion Leader's Job? D-3*, 3.

42   William F. Johnston, "Monthly Narrative Report of Extension Specialist, State Discussion Group Leader, June 1936, in Cooperative Extension Service Records, Box 2219, Folder 41, University Archives and Historical Collections, Michigan State University.

43   William F. Johnston, "Monthly Narrative Report of Extension Specialist, State Discussion Group Leader, June 1936," in Cooperative Extension Service Records (Box 22191936).

44   Carl F. Taeusch, "Memorandum to M. L. Wilson, October 4, 1935," in *Record Group* 16 (Box 7: Entry 33, Folder "School for Extension Workers", 1935). The Records of the Office of the Secretary of Agriculture, National Archives.

45   Gladys L. Baker, *The County Agent* (Chicago, IL: The University of Chicago Press, 1939), 85.

46   For example, see Charles Kenneth Roberts, *The Farm Security Administration and Rural Rehabilitation in the South* (Knoxville: University of Tennessee Press, 2015); Sam F. Stack Jr., *The Arthurdale Community School: Education and Reform in Depression Era Appalachia* (Lexington: The University Press of Kentucky, 2016).

47   Walter A. Rowlands, "Land Use Planning in Rural Areas: Discussion," *The Planners' Journal* 5, no. 1 (1939): 18.

48   C. V. Ballard, "Letter to A. Drummond Jones, July 12, 1938," in *Record Group* 83 (Box 623: Entry 19, Folder "Schools - Michigan", 1938), The Records of the Office of the Secretary of Agriculture, National Archives.

49   In his history about the first century of Michigan State University's existence, Madison Kuhn made a brief comment about discussion groups during this period of time. "Discussion groups were encouraged and discussion leaders were trained because the device proved effective in mobilizing community sentiment in favor of better living as well as better farming." Madison Kuhn, Michigan State: *The First Hundred Years, 1855-1955* (East Lansing: Michigan State University Press, 1955), 386.

50   Harry A. Overstreet and Bonaro W. Overstreet, *Town Meeting Comes to Town* (New York: Harper & Brothers, 1938); Christopher P. Loss, *Between Citizens and the State: The Politics of American Higher Education in the 20th Century* (Princeton: Princeton University Press, 2012), 85; William Keith and Paula Cossart, "The Search for 'Real'

Democracy: Rhetorical Citizenship and Public Deliberation in France and the United States, 1870-1940," in *Rhetorical Citizenship and Public Deliberation*, edited by Christian Kock and Lisa S. Villadsen (University Park, PA: Pennsylvania State University Press, 2012), 56.

[51] Shaffer, "Cultivating Deliberative Democracy through Adult Civic Education," 302.

[52] Johnston read widely about group discussion, an emerging topic of interest in the 1930s. In a monthly narrative report from 1936, he writes about the differences between public speaking and group discussion found in Lyman Spicer Judson, *A Manual of Group Discussion, Circular 446* (Urbana, IL: University of Illinois College of Agriculture Agricultural Experiment Station and Extension Service in Agriculture and Home Economics, 1936). William F. Johnston, "Monthly Narrative Report of Extension Specialist, State Discussion Group Leader, April 1936," in Cooperative Extension Service Records, Box 2219, Folder 41, University Archives and Historical Collections, Michigan State University.

[53] Carl F. Taeusch, "Freedom of Assembly," *Ethics* 63, no. 1 (1952): 41; "Division Activities—February, 1943," in *Record Group* 83 (Box 535: Entry 19, Folder "Division of Program Study and Discussion," 1943); David Lachman, "Democratic Ideology and Agricultural Policy 'Program Study and Discussion' in the U.S. Department of Agriculture, 1934-1946" (Master's Thesis, University of Wisconsin - Madison, 1991), 50; Gilbert, *Planning Democracy*, 142; Shaffer, "What Should You and I Do?" 141; "Cultivating Deliberative Democracy through Adult Civic Education"; Paul L. Vogt, "Study Clubs and Citizenship," *Mountain Life and Work* 15, no. 4 (1940): 6; A. Drummond Jones (1941); Farmer Discussion Is Adult Education, *Adult Education Bulletin*, 5(4): 121-125.

[54] Richard S. Kirkendall, *Social Scientists and Farm Politics in the Age of Roosevelt* (Columbia: University of Missouri Press, 1966), 195-261; Gilbert, *Planning Democracy*, 238-260.